THE

MAPMAKER

BY DAWN M HAFNER

YOUR 33 DAY JOURNEY TOWARDS DAILY
PRESENCE

THE MAPMAKER Copyright © 2017 by Dawn M Hafner

ISBN-13: 978-1544798554

ISBN-10: 1544798555

First Edition: March 2017

10 9 8 7 6 5 4 3 2 1

If you enjoy this book, please consider leaving a review on Amazon. Gratitude and love to you for spending your most precious resource with me, your time.

You can connect with me on Twitter @bewhereyouare1, Facebook at https://www.facebook.com/bewhereyouaredawn/**, or Instagram @be_where_you_are, or my website** www.dawnmhafner.com**.**

Contents

DEDICATION

Drew and Ethan,

I have learned more from you both than I've ever taught you. I will be forever grateful for the blessing of God allowing me the joy of being your mom on this journey. You know that I believe we picked each other. Thank you for choosing to share your journey with me.

Where ever you go in life, my heart is right there with you. You have all my love and support every day of your life. Always be true to yourself and you can never go wrong. God's truth comes through you when you are still enough to listen. I am so very proud of the men you are becoming. Thank you for loving me as only you can.

Love always,

Mom

CHARITABLE DONATION

50% of the profits from this book will be donated to Dress For Success.

You will see in a couple of the stories; abuse has touched my life. Because of this, I have a strong desire to want to help women empower themselves. This led me to volunteer at Dress For Success.

The mission of Dress for Success is to empower women to achieve economic independence by providing a network of support, professional attire, and development tools to help women thrive in work in life.

INTRODUCTION

Last year I went to see an alternative medicine type of doctor. He had helped my son Drew get through a difficult medical issue traditional medicine had failed to resolve. Drew had months of severe nerve pain in his hands and feet. These attacks would come almost daily in the evening and render him unable to enjoy his summer doing normal kid things. The attacks were brutal to watch. I was helpless to take away his pain. As a mom, seeing your child suffering and knowing you can't fix it brings such anger and despair.

This doctor had some unusual techniques, involving Drew holding vials of various elements while the doctor pushed on his limbs to test his energy. It was quite unusual, but he managed to cure what the traditional doctors could not. After two sessions of this treatment in the office the attacks stopped. I was once again reminded of how much we don't understand in this world. Just because I can't apply logic to how he was healed doesn't change the fact that he was healed.

Witnessing the power of his treatment sparked me to seek out an appointment with him for myself. I was interested in a simple wellness type of appointment. I didn't have any specific issues that needed solving. Part of his practice is the belief that all physical ailments are the manifestation of an emotional issue unresolved. And really, who doesn't have unresolved emotional issues? You're breathing, right?

Even though I didn't have any physical complaints, part way through the appointment he asked me rather bluntly, "What is it that you are afraid of?"

I answered the way most people would, by lying to both him and myself, and saying "Uh…nothing…?" *After all, I barely knew this guy. What am I going to say to such an odd question anyway?* I'm a fully functioning adult and mom, so I am pretty much fearless.

He gave me a look that said *get real please* and said "Now, let's try this again. What is it that you are afraid of?"

I thought to myself, w*ell, what do I have to lose here?* So, I responded with complete honesty, off the top of my head, and it all just poured out… "I am afraid I am not in the right spot in my life. I am afraid I am not living my destiny. I am afraid I'm not on the right path. Afraid I missed the instructions somehow to this life and I am way off from what I was sent here to do. Afraid I am failing at serving my purpose, not touching the lives I am supposed to or learning the lessons I need to. Not becoming all I was destined to be. Yes…that is exactly what I am afraid of."

"And so, who will judge if you did this right or did this wrong?" he asked.

"Well….God of course," I said quietly. "God will decide if I did it right or did it wrong."

He simply nodded. Only barely acknowledging my answer, leaving me to sit with my words, surrounding me that had just poured out into the room.

"What else are you afraid of?" he asked again.

Boy, this is a tough crowd, I thought. *Wasn't that answer deep enough?*

"I am afraid I'm screwing up my boys."

"Why?"

"The divorce. I carry a lot of guilt for creating pain for them. I am supposed to protect them from pain and instead my failure has caused them pain." The tears welled up despite my efforts to stop them.

"That's understandable."

He seemed satisfied to have some answers. Maybe the tears told him he'd pushed me far enough. He went on to have me hold vials and review a chart about how different emotions can show up in the body as particular ailments. He complimented me on my cognitive testing, saying that I scored better than anyone before in that area. He said I'm in very good health. *Great*, I thought when leaving. *I am in great health with the normal human baggage of guilt and fear of never being enough. I'm perfectly human.*

At some point in our lives most humans question, "Why am I here?" Once we wake up enough to confront that question, we search for answers nonstop for the rest of our lives. Maybe not daily, but the question comes up again, and again, and again. Some people search in religion. Some search in relationships. Some search in attaining goals in education or wealth. The search for our meaning unites us as humans. From the moment we realize the gap in understanding our existence, we spend the rest of our years trying on different attempts to fill that gap.

Life has a gap in it. It just does. You don't go crazy trying to fill it like some lunatic. – Take This Waltz

And yet as we are searching our way in this world, we also are taught that we should be magically found by someone else on their similar journey. We are taught that we are destined to find our soulmate, and that he or she will complete us. Something about our society and even most religions teach us that coupling up is the answer. We are expected to find love, get married, and have children. The end amen. Then as parents we turn around and encourage our children to follow the same search. We have massive parties to celebrate marriage. When doesn't anyone ever celebrate someone's decision to be single? Why isn't that also joyous?

We want to be swept off our feet with a great, deep, and genuine, intimate love given especially to us by our soulmate. We hope for a love so deep that it will complete us and be everything we've been seeking. We want to be made to feel whole by another. Even wedding bible readings preach about becoming one. So, of course we place our hope and faith in that path. Surely my life will be purposeful and meaningful if I can only find my soulmate.

Unhappy? Maybe you just haven't found the One yet, your friends will tell you. We hear encouragement to date and find the perfect mate for us. We search and search and perhaps find what we think will fill us up. Sometimes even those who don't find what they're searching for finally settle. The magical promise doesn't always feel like what we were told it should be. If we are being honest, we all know more miserable married people than happy ones. Yet, we still encourage others to follow the same path. What if we are looking for fulfillment and love in the wrong place? What if it doesn't exist outside of ourselves at all?

It's like playing the scratch-off lottery game from a pile of known losing cards. We scratch and scratch, hoping to hit a winner. We keep moving through the pile, discarding the cards that didn't bring us the jackpot. Moving through the entire stack, never knowing that it's guaranteed to not bring the instant prize we are hoping for. Each new card brings us a surge of excitement that maybe, just maybe, this will be the ONE! Sounds like dating, huh?

I'm not saying having an intimate relationship isn't an important part of life for most people. Who wants to travel this journey without significant human connection? But, as women we especially tend to wrap up our entire meaning around our significant relationship. We use it often to define ourselves and we are on a hunt for the perfect man.

I've watched girlfriends for years move through men. None of them quite the right fit. Disappointment abounds in all their lack. At the same time that they are searching for what they've been taught will bring them completeness, they downgrade other connections in their lives as less important. Many women have fulfilling, beautiful relationships with their children, girlfriends, parents, and siblings, and yet, if that illusive significant relationship is absent, life is somehow labeled a failure. Really? How can all the beauty be shunned? Who defined this as the ultimate goal for our lives, to find our soulmate?

What if what we are searching for isn't within any one person to find? Isn't that a lot of pressure to put on one person? Through no fault of theirs or of our own, what if that is not the design? How sad to find out at the end of the pile we could have saved all that empty hope if we knew where to look for love, fulfillment, purpose, and meaning.

Maybe we had it within us all along, but we were too afraid to look inside ourselves. Too afraid to look inside and witness the ragged edges of us that are not so loving. Witness the fear. Witness the guilt and self-doubt, looking beyond all of that to find the love within.

Another way we sabotage ourselves and live in dichotomy is the speed at which we live our lives. We try to live way too fast. We move so swiftly we can barely see the scenery moving past us. We attempt to accomplish so much, but we know in our hearts slowing down is the only true path to feeling a deeper connection.

We speed through life missing the moments, because we feel this sense of urgency sneaking up on us that we label as our own mortality. We are scared to death of our lack of permanence here, our lack of meaning. So, we run from it as we run through life. The urgency is exaggerated with each year that passes by as our perception of time speeds up. We want love, but we embrace our fear and hold it close to our hearts even though it hurts us and holds us prisoners every day.

Life is full of these dichotomies and many more. We are in a battle with ourselves and some days it feels like we are losing. We came into this world seeking to find our place. Our seeking journey will last as long as we have breath left in our lungs. To enjoy the journey and just be who you are, I am learning, is enough. I have taken steps on my life path that have taught me how to listen better to what we are here to learn.

My hope for you is that this book will give you a 'pause' button, letting yourself become more in touch with the thoughts that reside as soul truths for you. I believe that many of my soul truths explored in this book are human truths that connect us. Think of this book as a stopwatch resting in your hand. The 'pause,' after all, is what makes the music. Without the pause between the notes there would be no music. In writing without the pause of the comma or the period the words would be nearly impossible to find meaning in. We need to 'pause' in our lives to create the stillness needed to witness. Only when we are still enough to witness our lives can we know where we are in our journey.

Use this book as a time to quiet the world down so that you can begin to hear the messages designed just for your heart and your soul. My hope is that by sharing some of my personal life moments that have spoken to me that you may find a way to let in your personal unique moments to touch your soul and heal your heart.

My other hope with this book is that you will use it going forward as a compass in your life. Our life journey is less like following a GPS with specific instructions and coordinates than it is like using a compass in our hand to spot check our directional path. A compass tells us what general direction we are heading in, but doesn't give us strict turn-by-turn directions. A compass requires the traveler to hold it in their hand to use it interactively. There is a partnership between the compass and the traveler. A compass is not providing you exact coordinates, but rather the needle moves and vibrates as we move, guiding us gently towards the right direction we are being led.

Each short story or essay is an observation about everyday life moments I have found meaning within. Following each story is an invitation for you to explore your own life in that area, journaling some thoughts to guide your direction. The book covers topics including motherhood, friendship, marriage, divorce, childhood cancer, abuse, our own mortality, and life purpose. In sharing our own stories, we can release others from their own prison. There is power and healing in sharing. We learn when others share their own stories with us. My stories will be different than your stories. These are the lessons I have heard for me. You have your own to discover.

Journaling is a powerful form of learning, exploring, and even of prayer. The connection physically between the sensation of writing at your fingertips and the emotions pouring out into physical words holds a power unlike any other. I fully encourage you to do the journaling even if you don't consider yourself a writer. Writing with prompts is much easier to jump into than starting from a blank page. What you reflect on in the prompts will open up other areas of your curiosity to explore for your journey.

You will learn new things about yourself, things you didn't know you needed to grow forward on your journey. Journaling seems to magically bring to the surface what needs to be examined. Journaling also gives you permission to release the weight of that which weighs you down as it's no longer trapped within you.

So, I urge you to grab a spiral notebook or if you prefer a pretty journal you may have long ago stuffed in a drawer, waiting for the encouragement to use. Reading my stories is only using this book halfway. The journaling on your own life experiences is where the real magic lies.

The book is organized into thirty-three days. Why did I choose thirty-three? The number thirty-three in the bible is thought to be connected to the promises of God. That is what I believe presence does for us. It allows us to hear God's intention for us, His promise to us. He is trying to communicate with us all day, every day. We must slow down to hear Him.

I recommend exploring just one story and journaling exercise each day. Slowing down the pace of how fast you absorb these stories will enable you to witness how each theme shows up for you in your life. You will have thirty-three days to explore your thoughts as they come to you, and you'll begin to notice yourself responding to similar situations in your own life that will bring new perspective for you personally. This is a gift of intentional presence you are investing in for yourself.

The time commitment for each day is less than half an hour of reading and journaling. Then you will want to tune into the theme during your day as you notice your own moments speaking to you. Watch around you during the day for your own stories surrounding you to reveal at the right time to you the magical, teaching moments in your own life.

Through reading, journaling, and your own daily focus you will be in partnership with your compass. I view tuning into our compass as our responsibility in this journey to actively respond to direction. I am reminded often however that the map on which we travel is not our map. We must overall trust the mapmaker in God and know that he is the maker of our map. He has designed us for his purpose. He has plans for each one of us, plans that include every experience we've ever had to form and shape us into what role we are meant to serve here.

While we use the stopwatch for pause and the compass for tuning into our directions, they are mere tools to reveal God's map that he has made especially for us.

I went to Catholic school from kindergarten through high school graduation. The language of religion and speaking of God has come naturally for me due to my life experiences from when I was a child. Not everyone was raised that way. If you are nondenominational or even someone who considers yourself more spiritual than religious I still speak your language.

Inclusiveness is something I value deeply. There are many paths to the same place. My path was born of my experiences, but that doesn't mean there are not other paths. If the word God to describe the energy, goodness, light, the universe, love, nature, and the source of all of creation just doesn't resonate for you, that doesn't exclude us from still connecting.

Even if you use a different word than me we are still speaking of the same. Humans developed language and the system of letters, sounds and words. The fact that you may find a different combination of letters, sounds and words to describe the same Higher Power that I describe as God doesn't mean we have no connection to share. It means we are simply on slightly different paths leading to the same place. We share more in common than we do differences. While I use the word God freely it is important for me to let my value of inclusivity be known to you the reader. Nonjudgement is one of the big themes that comes through in this book. So, if my openness to all forms of spirituality and religion turns you off, I'd encourage you to ponder the role that inclusivity and openness plays in your religion.

If you are ready to put fear aside, and take this journey of self-discovery with me, grab your journal and open to Day One. When you first go to journal and if your pen is silent at first, that is just fear showing up. There is nothing to fear here. Only good can come from knowing yourself more deeply and hearing the messages God has designed for you.

DAY ONE

BE WHERE YOU ARE

I was irritated and rushed, a normal state of being for a mom with young children. Trying to balance the new-mom life was like being plunged into a cold-water bath that you never had any relief from. I desperately wished to be a mom. I went back to school for a second degree and made sure we were financially stable and ready for children before we began our family. By the time that happened I was already thirty. Being well into adulthood and having been responsible for myself essentially since my first year of college, I felt as ready as I thought possible. I was a planner. I laugh now thinking back to how much of my life I planned and how opposite it looks now.

Nothing can prepare you for what it's like when you cross over into your new life as mom. It is miraculous, it is beautiful, it is poetic, it is everything I hoped it to be. It is also twenty-four-hour nonstop madness at this incredible pace of things to do and items to take care of on literally no sleep. The lack of sleep goes on for years while you attempt to look human at work with spit and milkish-colored vomit on your classy black blazer – nearly a daily occurrence. At home I would call sweats and Iowa college T-shirts a wardrobe. It is a magical, messy, blurry disaster. I remember being so fearful as a new mom that I couldn't even take a shower without my husband home to watch the baby for those ten minutes. Eventually I graduated to placing the bouncy seat on the bathroom floor and peeking out of my shower every minute to check on the baby. In the midst of this fearful, joyous life, many of us are also tasked with how to still push forward to succeed at our careers. No one can detect any decrease in focus or performance or being a mom has surely interfered with your work. Then you also have to be the sweet, sexy wife that your husband fell for before all this needy, intense chaos took his wife away from focusing on him. I'm exhausted just thinking about it!

So, there I was, age 33, with Ethan in a stroller and Drew on my hip. I was tasked with gift shopping for a wedding we had to go to later that day. Just the thought of getting these two charming young men dressed into wedding appropriate clothes created a feeling of exhaustion. It would be no small feat. I'd be required to also get myself in the same state of all dolled up and dressed up. That was my task for later, after this errand. I was tired from the night before with no sleep. I was ticked off that I had to not only run this errand, but drag the boys in tow as well. And, we were out of town at a mall that I wasn't familiar with.

There I stood at the mall map sign with my personal handsome little circus. I tried to figure out what was open and which shops would have something appropriate and affordable. I pointed to the map to show my son Drew where we were.

"See, this red X means we are here on the map, and we need to go over here to this side," I explained. He seemed interested enough, so I was briefly satisfied that I had passed on some tiny bit of learning for the day. When we turned our little circus around to head away from the map kiosk, Drew shouted, "Bee mom! Bee! Look, a bee on Where We Are!" I briefly glanced in that direction – enough to satisfy him – and said, "Yes, honey. A bee on the map. Let's go."

As I shopped I could hear him in the stroller repeating, "Bee on Where We Are, Mom…..Bee Where We Are, Mom…"

Later that evening, I frantically got everyone ready for the wedding. I decided I would not have the time necessary to curl my hair ever again in my life. Then I heard it again.

"Bee Where We Are." I stopped. I pondered that sentence and repeated it in my head….BE Where You Are. BE Where You Are…..*hmmm, as in live here, live now, and live in this moment. Interesting. And not what I've been living. Don't think about the to-do list that you have to tackle Sunday night when you get home before a full work week starting early Monday morning. Think about this moment, right here, right now. You are here having a weekend away to see old friends and celebrate one of the great moments of life with the amazing miracles that God has entrusted you with. Pay attention. Wake up and see what you have before you at this very moment. Stop letting your mind steal away your moments. You can't get them back.*

That was the beginning of what still is my personal daily mantra: Be Where You Are.

There is an appropriate time for everything under the sun. As written in Ecclesiastes 3, (or quoted in the movie Footloose – take your pick): "A time to kill and a time to heal; A time to tear down and a time to build up. A time to weep and a time to laugh; A time to mourn and a time to dance."

There is a time for everything that we humans are here on earth to experience. Our lives can be much more peaceful and joy-filled if we only surrender ourselves to the time we are in and allow ourselves to Be Where We Are in every moment.

Ever have a day off with your kids, enjoying the day fully when you suddenly feel that tug of work pulling on you? You view them watching a movie and think..."*Hmmm....well maybe while they are doing this I can just finish up that one last project that I didn't get to that was overdue.*" So, you do it. You pull out the work when you had planned to take the day off to spend it with them. At the end of the day, how do you feel? Do you feel good for accomplishing more than most mothers could? Fabulous for being such a dedicated rock star at work, working even on your day off?

Probably not. Chances are you feel like you did a half-ass job being a mom and being a professional that day. Chances are the kids did notice that you checked out during the movie. And truth be known, chances are that wasn't your best client work that day either. You feel like you failed on both fronts, giving neither your best effort.

This struggle for balance and harmony and trying to be everything to everyone all the time was something that plagued me so much during my early motherhood years. I felt like a constant failure. I was no longer able to dedicate sixty hours at work to attempt to be a star performer. I also held myself to high standards as a mom. I read probably twenty parenting books on how to do everything just right. I multi-tasked like a rock star and people would marvel at how much I could accomplish and keep all these balls in the air. You know what? It was exhausting. You know what? It was fake. No one can do it all, and holding out the false premise that you, unlike the rest of the population, can do it all is a lie. You can't be a star at everything. And, believe it or not, if you don't devote time to yourself for sleep, exercise, and self-care, you will fail every person and every goal that you hold dear.

The one thing that really helped me get some sense of control over this constant do-more-be-more attitude that is forced upon us was this mantra that I repeated numerous times throughout the day in my head. *BE* Where You *ARE*. That's it. Just *BE*, fully and genuinely immerse yourself in being right where you *ARE*. Don't listen to the tug trying to call you away from your present moment. You will never get this very moment again in your life. Your loved ones will never again look exactly as they do right at this moment. Be in it. Be in it fully and completely. Immerse yourself in it. Surrender yourself to it. Fully be present.

You must give yourself the credit that to this point you have made some good basic decisions about what kind of job you will maintain and how much time you have to devote to your family. Give yourself some trust and credit to follow that. When you are at your job and you feel that guilty tug that you should be with your children, stop. Stop and redirect your thoughts. Choose to BE where you are. You are at work, and the only thing you can do is fully BE present where you are. Do it and you will feel energized and better about your work performance.

Do the same thing at home. The next time you are enjoying downtime with your kids and feel guilty for time wasted watching Dora the Explorer and feeling like you should grab your phone, stop. Stop and redirect your thoughts. Choose to BE where you are fully. You are with the precious loves of your life and they will notice you fully engaging in this time. And you will feel tons better about your parenting.

Juggling parenting and other responsibilities is not the only place applying this practice of full presence can be helpful. We put ourselves in two different places mentally when facing other struggles as well.

Another example is choosing to give up an entire day or a string of days, or months, or sometimes years to your anger and hurt. When you are angry at someone, how much time do you spend thinking about that? Do you go over and over the entire event or conversation repeatedly? Maybe it consumes you, eats you alive. What happens to that day for you? Are you living in a past moment every day of your life? You can never get that time back. Yes, we will have events that will stir up anger and hurt us. The faster we can forgive, however, the sooner we can BE in the moment we are presently in and grow and learn from witnessing our current moment fully. Withholding forgiveness will rob you of your precious time and divert you from your journey.

You must forgive those that hurt you, even if whatever they did to you is unforgivable in your mind. You will forgive them not because they deserve to be forgiven, but because you don't want to suffer and hurt yourself every time you remember what they did to you. Forgiveness is your own mental healing. Forgiveness is an act of self-love. – Don Miguel Ruiz

It sounds simple, but, believe me, it is so powerful. Give yourself permission and train your mind to fully BE where you are. You may have to retrain and redirect your mental tapes one hundred and fifty times in one day, but eventually you will find a more peaceful balance that exists first within your own mind. That will extend out to your entire life and the lives of those you love.

"BE".....where you ARE. Try it in your life and see what kind of effect it has on your state of mind. That is what this book is about...not doing a perfect job, but a better job at just that concept of BE Where You Are.

Feel your soul slow down enough to catch more of those teachable moments that are sent to us to form and shape our hearts and lives – the moments that reveal to us the purpose of our journey here.

JOURNAL PROMPTS

Think about the different aspects of your life – family, career, significant other or spouse, spirituality, health, self-care, etc. Which aspects of your life cause you the most conflict? What do you feel you are sacrificing at the expense of another aspect of your life?

When you struggle to balance these conflicting areas of life, how does that show up for you? What thoughts repeat themselves? What physical symptoms do you experience? Where do you go in your mind when you feel that pressure? Do you get angry, feel shame, or close down? What is your go-to move when confronted with the conflict? What does your self-talk sound like in these moments?

When you witness this conflict showing up for you, what new loving response will you replace your old thoughts with? Consciously try on a new focused thought each time as a response to the conflict and journal your experience.

DAY TWO

SEE THE JOY THROUGH PAIN

This last Fourth of July, a friend and I had drinks at our local sports bar and intended to eat there. Since the bar was so busy, we finished our drinks and headed up the street to the small town ice cream shop for sandwiches instead. It was a gorgeous sunny day with a perfectly comfortable temperature. The entire town seemed to be buzzing with holiday activity.

We reached the door to come in at the same time that an elderly woman and her husband were coming out. My friend and I both had the same reaction, to widely hold the door back and allow them to make their way out. I noticed the husband was using a walker. Even with that assistance, it was a significant and painfully slow process for him to make it out the door.

"I'm sorry we are so slow, dear," the wife apologized.

"You are just fine," I replied. "We are in no hurry. Please take all the time you need."

I smiled at her while she waited patiently for her husband. She reached forward and put both of her hands onto my hands, which were holding the door, and said, "I sure hope if you're ever eighty-four and have Parkinson's that someone is there to hold the door for you."

I looked into her eyes and smiled again, then said "I certainly hope so too."

"I hope you have a nice day," I wished both of them. I watched them make the slow, agonizing journey to their silver Buick from the last decade, my heart tugging out of my chest to follow them.

My friend and I went inside and ordered our sandwiches. After we sat down at our table, I looked out the window wistfully. My mind kept wandering back to that couple. It had to have been quite the effort for them to journey outside of the house at all based on what I'd seen. And yet somehow, despite the obstacles, they found it in themselves to venture out for a small lunch to celebrate the Fourth of July.

I felt beauty in the small moment I had with the woman, when she touched my hands and wished me well far into my distant future. I wondered if the she saw the beauty in that moment, too, or if the pain she and her husband had to carry was so great that beauty was just too hard to find.

That got me thinking about how difficult it can be for people who are struggling so hard with something in life to see anything beyond their pain. I know when I have experienced my lowest of lows that beauty is hard to uncover through the pain. When you are dealing with things that weigh your heart down so deeply, it can feel like you are at the bottom of a fifty-foot dark well with no steps to get out and no light to see from the bottom. It can be hard to even get out of bed and be functional on some days.

How many of us are missing the beauty because of the pain? Pain can envelop us like a wet, weighted blanket that is so twisted and tangled we can't shake it off no matter how hard we try. After so many attempts, we start to get weak from the effort. How much time do we waste wrestling with pain and missing the beauty around us? It makes my heart ache to that so many people are missing so much.

The positive light is that there is a way out of the pain, like a rope thrown down into the well for help, and anyone can grasp onto it. That rope out can be as simple as ….helping another person. The way out of pain can be that simple. Reach out and muster the energy to do one simple, small thing for someone else. Cut some flowers and bring them to a neighbor. Bake cookies for a friend. Smile at a stranger, or volunteer to let someone go first in the grocery line. These simple acts of kindness take us out of our well of pain and into the light of day, even into someone else's day.

Doing good for others is the most powerful painkiller for us. We can often muster up the strength for someone else that we can't find to give ourselves.

The most beautiful thing about this truth is that two people in pain actually have the power to lift each other up, even though neither has the strength to lift themselves up alone. Reach out – help someone so that you can take that first step out of your pain and stop missing the beauty that is passing you by.

Walk together. Feel the heart beats. Experience the presence. This is how to be thankful. — Amit Ray

JOURNAL PROMPTS

We all have pain in our lives. What painful areas in your life have kept you weighed down for too long, or come back to weigh down your spirit too often?

What techniques have you used in the past to work through the painful parts of your life? How effective have you found those techniques to be in working you through those painful times?

If you have pain you're facing now or if thoughts of past pain come to you today, respond by choosing to do an act of kindness for someone. In addition, if you aren't struggling with something painful, tune in more acutely to those around you. Watch for people who seem to be struggling. Reach out to them with an act of kindness, no matter how simple. Journal your acts of kindness and reflections.

DAY THREE

30,000 FEET OF PERSPECTIVE

I t had been a lovely Mother's Day. The May weather was gorgeous and sunny, yet still cool enough to enjoy – a promising reminder that Spring had finally arrived. I had enjoyed church with my husband and boys followed by a delicious brunch buffet in our small rural Iowa town. The only problem was that it was too short; I had to excuse myself from brunch early to catch a flight.

My work required me to be at a conference the next week, starting on Monday morning early. On the long drive to the airport, I muttered under my breath about what a royal jerk the man in charge was. Anyone who planned to attend the conference was required to fly in the Sunday night of Mother's Day to make the first meeting. I wondered, *who does that? Doesn't he have a mother?* I was upset for me and my boys to have to cut Mother's Day short.

To top it all off, it was predicted to be a stormy night and I have never been a huge fan of flying. The flight from Chicago started off smoothly, but as we drew closer to Washington, D.C., the lightning started and the wind began throwing the small plane around. We experienced quite a few 'joy stick' drops, what feels like the pilot is intentionally jerking the control stick down while we're falling thousands of feet through an air pocket.

To this day I still think of it as the scariest flight I have ever been on. As the weather intensified, every person around me seemed to have a different reaction. Some held on fiercely to the arm rests. A few people appeared to be reading, but I doubt they truly were with all those bumps we experienced. A mom held her child on her lap. She appeared to be attempting to soothe herself as much as to calm the little boy.

From the row behind me, I heard a woman sobbing out loud.

"Oh, dear God, heavenly Father, help us. Our Father, who art in heaven. Hallowed be thy name…" She prayed out loud while she cried.

Then the plane dropped again.

"Oohh, God help me….Thy will be done on earth as it is in heaven. Give me this day…"

Over and over, she sobbed and repeated the prayer. Crying, praying.

I thought, *maybe I should be more scared than I am!*

This was not a good combination – the plane bumping and dropping, the woman crying and praying, the stale air thick and tense.

I silently wished she would stop. She was certainly not helping the situation. Her frightened voice and sobbing added to the atmosphere of fear, making it all seem more surreal and as if something bad really was about to happen. I felt my own tension rise, wondering if it was worse than I thought. The large air drops continued while the weather threw us around in the stormy sky. I wondered if we might not make it. Then, suddenly, I heard something quite unexpected break the thick tension.

"Wheee!!!!! Whooo Hoooo!!!!! Wheeee!!!!! Do it again!!!!" a little girl's voice shrieked.

This was followed by her mom saying, "Shush….be quiet darling, people are uneasy, honey."

"Wheee!!!!! Whooo Hoooo!!!!! Wheeee!!!!! Do it again!!!!" she repeated, doing as little girls will do, ignoring her mom.

I couldn't help myself from laughing right straight out loud.

How beautiful a lesson there was before us. We had one woman trying to pray her way out of a certain early death, and one row over in the same exact set of circumstances was a child showing complete and utter joy that she literally could not bear to contain. She was enjoying the thrilling ride of her life that she didn't want to ever stop.

Two different people, the same exact circumstances – a perfect example of how much your perspective matters. Yes, the little girl was absent of the adult knowledge of how bad the result could have been. But what good is knowledge if we only use it for negativity? Both the woman and the little girl were influencing others. Which one would spread joy and bring smiles? Which one would bring dread and fear? Both were affecting others on the plane in two very opposite ways.

It made me think about my own perspective. Was I a woman who had her Mother's Day unfairly cut short, or was I simply a very blessed woman to have the opportunity to even be a mother and spend time with those I love most? Was I a woman robbed of my Sunday by some crappy job requirement, or was I a woman proud and happy of my career that had blessed me and my family with many opportunities? Was I going to spread negativity or joy?

What is your perspective doing to you and those around you? If you are experiencing negativity and blaming your circumstances, take another look. Is the filter through which you are viewing flawed? How could you look at the situation differently and use it to bring more grace and love to yourself and others?

No two persons ever read the same book. — *Edmund Wilson*

JOURNAL PROMPTS

In what areas of life do you struggle to maintain a positive perspective? Often we find ourselves to be positive in certain situations or areas but negative in others.

Think of one person you know who has faced some significant hardships in their life and yet always seems to stay positive to the point that you are amazed at their positive perspective. How do they display their perspective to you or others? What does this person do differently or believe differently than others to make them stand out to you as having excellent perspective?

Identify instances when you feel yourself struggling with negativity. Once you identify the negativity, ask yourself, what would the person you've identified do or believe about this situation? How does that differ from your normal actions or thoughts? Which response do you find more helpful for your day?

DAY FOUR

YOU MATTER

When I was at the elementary school age, Dad went around to different nursing homes on Sundays after church. He was not a pastor, but a lay person trained to give the holy communion. At each home he gave a blessing to the elderly and brought the Holy Communion to those who couldn't get to church. I would watch as Dad spoke the words, "The body of Christ." Those who were able would respond, "Amen." They would take the host the old-fashioned way – directly placed onto their tongues. They didn't know that people had started doing this differently in church, with the priest placing the host into the person's hands for them to place it into their mouths themselves. At the nursing homes, Dad often broke the hosts into smaller pieces as several of the elderly couldn't manage to take the entire host and chew it all.

I had a special friend at the Lutheran Home. Her name was Margaret. Every time Dad and I came into her room, she seemed to be waiting for us to arrive.

"Oh, I'm so glad to see you!" she would greet us with her quivering voice. "I have saved some candy back for you." She'd pull some variety of hard candies from the pocket of her smock. When it was time for us to leave, she would beg us to stay. We'd always stay just a little bit longer.

Sometimes she tried to give me things that were larger gifts, like a stuffed animal or a pretty glass dish. My dad would refuse, even though I secretly would have loved to have some of her treasures to take home. They would have reminded me of her.

I was devastated the day we went to her room and were told she had passed on that week. I had wondered, *how was it possible? She was here the last time we came, and now she's gone? Forever.* My experiences with these visits became my first lessons about death.

Those childhood memories encouraged me to volunteer for hospice as an adult. We volunteered as a family, and my hope was to pass on the gift of service to Drew and Ethan. We had a couple regular patients we would go see together once a week. The boys were not asked to visit anyone close to passing on. I wanted this to be an enriching experience appropriate for their ages. The visits for them were just like visiting someone in the nursing home.

One day I was called to see a hospice patient who I didn't normally see. The boys weren't with me that day. The nursing home where she resided happened to be on my way home from my job in town. She was in pretty bad shape. Her family needed to leave for a bit and wanted someone to be with their mom so she wasn't left alone at all. They knew she was very close to passing on. I was available, so I stepped in. I had never met the woman or her family before.

When I walked into the small barren room, I was taken aback by how pale she was. Her skin was as stark white as her hair. I was told she was mostly blind. She couldn't look at me or talk to me or smile at me. When I held her hand, she couldn't even squeeze my hand. No one else was around, just me and her. I'd never seen her before in my entire life. Total strangers.

I read a book to her that I adore and had with me, *The Alchemist*. Despite the fact that all of her senses were unusable, I could still sense that my being there meant something to her. She turned her head slightly as I read aloud. I could sense her breathing slowing some, like a tension was easing. Her presence was acknowledging my presence. Her small movements showed me that she had interest in someone taking interest in her, that someone was there for her and comforting her. I let our connection hang heavy in the air as I read aloud, holding her hand, and looking into eyes that couldn't see me. But I knew she could feel me.

As I read, I felt the realization of a universal truth that we are all human. We are all connected – even strangers – through the human and spiritual experience of being. We are all on this journey at the same time, even if we only overlap for a short while.

Giving someone your simple, attuned presence is the most authentic spiritual gift you can ever give. Anyone can give this. You don't have to be good-looking. You don't have to be witty, charming, or the life of the party. You don't have to dress nice or be outgoing or charismatic. You don't need to be smart, sexy, or young. You don't need to be any of these things to bring joy, love, peace, and comfort to another human being.

All you have to bring is yourself and your heart. All by yourself, just being yourself, doing nothing other than being present in the moment for someone who needs someone, anyone, to show up for them. God showed me in that moment that I mattered. You know what else? You matter. You matter more than you can ever imagine in the most farfetched corners of your imagination. You matter just as you are, right here, right now. You don't need to achieve spectacular feats to make a difference in this world. You already are a spectacular feat. Simply show up as you are and reach out with all you have to someone who is in need on this journey. It's that simple. You matter that much to this world.

I don't care what the stars say about how small we are. One, even the smallest, weakest, most insignificant one, matters. — Rick Yancey

JOURNAL PROMPTS

Think back about the people you have known best in your life: Who always made you feel special when you were in their presence? It may have been a grandparent, parent, or special friend.

Journal about how it made you feel to be with them. What emotions come to mind when you reflect on being with them? What qualities did these people have that others didn't, that made you feel this way around them? How did they speak, listen, or behave around you?

From this list of qualities that made being in their presence so meaningful, select one to focus on today for yourself. Tune into that special quality, and witness when you see that quality in other people or in yourself. It could be a sense of calmness. It could be silliness. It could be the act of remembering small details about you. Notice and celebrate that special authentic gift when it presents itself to you.

DAY FIVE

A SILENT CRY FOR HELP – A PEEK INSIDE VERBAL ABUSE

The story you are about to read is true. It happened not to me, but to a close friend of mine. It is a story that needs to be shared.

Maggie was starting to breathe a little easier. They were at least in the car, the entire family loaded up and on their way to what she hoped would be a vacation full of good memories. They needed this. She needed this. She had worked very hard this week to get everything just right.

The laundry is all caught up, the travel food is purchased, backpacks and luggage are packed. The house is immaculate. The bills are paid. Nothing can possibly be overlooked. And so far, it appears she is successful. Her husband seems pleased, and she hopes to keep it that way. She glances at Scott, and smiles as he drives.

They make their first stop for gas. Maggie and all three kids get out to use the restroom and grab some snacks while Scott pumps the gas. When they exit the store, they notice car is pulled up front for them; Scott is waiting. Maggie helps all the kids get settled back in, holding soda cups and snacks while seat belts are bucked up.

She settles in the front seat herself, buckles up and takes out the M&Ms she bought for herself. She offers some to her husband. In return he gives her a grunt of utter disgust and says, "Really? Do you really think you should be eating those?" Maggie feels her face turn flush, and the kids in the back fall quiet at the tone they often dread from their father. He continues on with disgust in his voice: "I watched you walk into the store, Maggie. You are barely able to fit into those shorts. I could not be more disappointed in you."

Maggie feels the one M&M melting against the roof of her mouth, and it is enough to make her want to vomit. Not again. She did everything right, so right. She feels three sets of eyes from the back seat looking at her for what she's going to do. "I'm sorry, Scott," she muffles out softly.

"SORRY! You're sorry?! God help us, I'm the one that's sorry for your worthless effort as a wife and mother. I do everything for this family. Everything! The least you can do is keep the house, the kids, and yourself looking decent. You disgust me. Sorry kids, but we need to go home. Your mom needs to spend some time working on herself. Your mom doesn't deserve a vacation."

Scott turns the car around the way they came, and, in silence, they drive back home. Maggie knows not to cry. That will only make matters worse. She is cursing herself for being in this marriage. Cursing herself for not getting it right. Cursing herself for being alive.

The kids try to scatter when they get in the house, but Scott stops them. "Nope, guys, not going anywhere. We are going to sit here and watch mom do a workout video. Something she should have been doing for weeks, clearly. Sit down."

Scott puts in a DVD and tells Maggie, "You need to show these kids by example what a good wife and woman does. DO IT. NOW!"

She has no choice. With shame, and avoiding eye contact with any of her children, she gets on the floor. With a stoic face, she completes the workout video. Her heart is breaking into pieces for her children. It's not that hard to keep from crying, though. After all these years, it's like the tears inside have dried up. Everything inside is stone, a numbness no one could understand. Another failure. And she really thought she had done everything right this time. She is so ashamed of the life she has given her kids.

* * * *

Maggie is a close friend of mine, and I watched her struggle with abuse for far too long. Sometimes I pushed her to take action. Sometimes I didn't for fear that she'd shut me out. I often ask myself now, *did I do enough? How could I have done more?*

From the outside looking in, it's easy for those who have not experienced this type of abuse to find themselves bewildered. People might ask, *Why doesn't she just walk out?* Having also been in an abusive relationship early in my adulthood, I do have some insight into how someone gets to this place.

The first time it happened to me, I don't think it even settled in for a day or so. We were in a fight about something when suddenly his hands were wrapped tightly around my neck. I was pinned up against the wall. He didn't hit me, but it didn't stop there.

He never struck me by hand. Most of the time, he shoved and pushed me into walls or furniture. He would pin me against a wall beyond my will, or throw me head first into a headboard, resulting in a bloody nose. One time in the middle of a fight, he suddenly took the shotgun down from the wall. There is nothing like seeing your partner grab a gun during a fight.

Those were the physical things. The verbal attacks were just as damaging.

"You'll never amount to anything."

"If it wasn't for your long hair, you wouldn't be even remotely attractive. Don't ever cut it, or you'll be nothing."

"Gee, looks like you've lost some weight. I think your ass seems less wide than normal."

Fear, control, manipulation, and threats were a part of my daily life. Combine all that joy with his late nights out drinking, and you may wonder why I didn't go running for the door, right? What's wrong with women (or men) who stay in these relationships anyway?

Nothing. Well, nothing at the start other than a good heart, a bend towards forgiveness, and searching for love in the wrong place. When you've endured this type of relationship for any length of time, a lot of damage is done. When you are beat down emotionally, mentally, and often physically for any length of time, it causes you to doubt your independence, your intelligence, and your very worth as a human being.

It took me a year and a half to finally get the strength to exit that relationship and a lifetime to work on the lessons from that experience. So, who am I to fault Maggie for the length of time it took her? Who are we to judge anyone unless we've lived their life?

Judging isn't the issue to examine. The question is, what can we do to help? This type of verbal abuse happens in more relationships than you might think. Maybe you have a friend who you think is clearly with the wrong person, someone who does not treat your friend with value. There's nothing horrible that you've witnessed firsthand, but more of a gut feeling you have from being around them. You notice something off in how your friend acts or talks. Maybe you can even identify with Maggie from a current or previous relationship.

What you can do for our friends in these situations is open up and be real with them about your concerns. Ask them if they are struggling, and let them know you will be there to help them. Let them know that you will listen without judgment. Let them know that sometimes bouncing things off another person can add perspective to a situation you've been in for a long time. Show them that gentle, unconditional love and support exists in you.

Maggie is terrified to open up to her family and friends, because she is fearful of how they will judge her as a person and a mother. She is also afraid that her friends and family will all abandon her if she isn't strong enough to leave Scott yet. And of course she is afraid of Scott's reaction if she trusts the wrong person and that trust is broken. Maggie is not on solid ground and may not even be able to make healthy decisions due to the abuse. She needs you to be strong for her and put aside your own fear. Put aside your own discomfort and your own reservations to take a risk.

Lend her a hand up by continuing your message of being there for her and encouraging her to take steps towards getting help. You may have to repeat your message of love and support for a long period of time before she believes she can grasp onto it.

To some of you, this situation may seem unfathomable, but verbal and physical abuse happens gradually. It's a little episode here, another small one there, mixed with good-intentioned forgiveness and hope. There is an illusion created over time implying that the victim has the power to control these outcomes by doing things "right." It is a sick, often long, and destructive, repetitive cycle that deteriorates more over time with many victims in its wake.

If you have a friend whom you suspect is in need, you won't regret stepping up and offering to be the first one to talk to about it. You won't regret pledging your loyalty and support. You might be the only one who does help and exactly the one she needs right now.

Be brave. Be vocal. Be there, and reach out with a heart full of love. Tell her you are there for her over and over again until she is ready to reach out. She will need you to make the change in her life. Your offer to help her and be there when she is ready will be a gift she carries with her. We can't live others' lives for them, and it hurts when we see our friends struggling, unhappy, and unsafe. We can stand ready and remind them often how worthy they are of a better life. We can show them that we will be their strength and walk with them through it all.

I wondered about her chicken-and-egg relationship with Dad. Which came first? Her helplessness or his controlling? — Justina Chen, North of Beautiful

JOURNAL PROMPTS

What would you do if Maggie was your friend? How far would you push her to take action? How involved would you get? What steps would you take?

How would your response change if she threatened to cut off ties with you altogether if you did something drastic, knowing you are the only friend she has confided in? What would you do if she never takes your advice, refusing to take action?

Think back through your life experiences. Identify any situations where you felt that something was off but have regrets about how you responded. It could be something you witnessed in public, such as a parent disciplining their child in an aggressive manner. It could be a friend of yours who you suspected of struggling with an eating disorder, alcoholism, or drug abuse. The world is full of people fighting battles. We will stand witness to them. What can you decide now that will prepare you to take action and support the victims to the best of your ability in the future?

DAY SIX

SILENT INSPIRATION

I've been attending what feels like endless track meets for the past couple of months. Most evenings are spent waiting for the next event one of my sons is in, watching a quick, race, then more waiting. These are some long, late nights. I love the atmosphere at the track and road races in general. There is a feeling you get there of comradery and supportiveness.

I grew up in a running family. At one time in college, I faithfully attended the YMCA gym on a daily basis. A girlfriend and I had a pact that we'd meet each other at six a.m. each morning and take turns driving to the gym. We had this routine for months. My friend was a stair-master fan, and I just loved to run. Winter in Iowa meant that you ran inside.

I'd head up to the track that was above the open gymnasium. It wasn't a large track; I think you had to make about twelve laps to get a mile in. The sides were slanted slightly inward at the outer lanes and you could look down at the gym below.

I had started running one particular morning, and shortly after I could feel the presence of someone pulling in behind me. Another runner, a man, was cruising about fifteen yards behind me. He settled in and stayed there, right behind me, keeping me from dragging down my pace. I could hear his feet pounding, his presence pushing me. I didn't like getting passed.

I saw that gentleman frequently when I went to the gym. I'd run my miles and he'd run right behind me like that. Often times he would still be running when I left. He was quite a bit older than I was, I'd guess by about twenty years. I was probably twenty-one years old at the time. This wasn't a case of him hitting on me in a sexual way, or anything like that. He clearly had no intention of exchanging conversation. We were both there to run...and run hard.

I kept coming to the gym, kept running my laps, and we kept pushing each other. Sometimes I led. Sometimes he led and I paced him. We never ran opposite sides but always near each other. We both knew we were making each other better and pushing each other harder. We'd both come and go, never exchanging a word, or even introducing ourselves. We were there to run and we used each other to get better.

I often thought that exchange was a bit strange but also, in hindsight, oddly beautiful – two strangers sharing a common interest, doing what they love with no other agenda than to work to the best of their abilities. No conversation. No explanation. Just running and pushing, using, and growing – a complete understanding – knowing that we were doing the same thing to each other and for each other. He made me a better runner that year. I'd like to think I did the same for him. I often wish I'd had a chance to at least say thanks, but, like many chapters in life, you don't get a forewarning when a chapter is about to come to a close. It simply closes and life moves on.

We don't have to speak eloquent speeches to inspire others. It can be as simple as showing up and doing what you do by just being you. It can be as simple as letting someone else silently push you and inspire you or exchanging those gifts with others by sharing our presence. It was a beautiful, human, pure exchange of gifts and spirit. And I still remember it as an experience which taught me that inspiring and connecting with others is attained by being yourself and showing up fully.

Think about who is surrounding you. Who is absorbing your spirit and gifts without you even being aware? Who are you silently inspiring? Who is lifting you up with their mere presence?

If you have someone like that in your life, I encourage you to say something before that chapter moves on, closing itself without warning.

THE MAPMAKER

The best and most beautiful things in the world cannot be seen or even touched. They must be felt with the heart. — Helen Keller

JOURNAL PROMPTS

Who in your life, past or present, have you've silently admired for their qualities? What did they teach you and how did they teach it? What effect did this have on your life?

Examine your own life now. Who in your circle of influence do you think you may be having an indirect but important impact on and how? What can you do to reach out to that person and help them even more?

After you have identified a few people who have shown you silent inspiration in your own life, narrow your list down to one. Write a hand-written thank-you note to this person expressing your gratitude for inspiring you and sharing their gifts. Mail the thank-you card to them. The gifts of this will amaze you and cause a rip effect you can't imagine.

DAY SEVEN

RECEIVING WITH GRACE

I was raised like many of you, at least I imagine. I was taught to be self-reliant, to take care of my responsibilities, and to give to others. I was taught to be responsible for myself – pay my own way, buy my own necessities, get myself to where I needed to be, be willing to notice others and lend a hand.

Sounds like a good thing, right? And it is, but...something is missing in that formula.

It came to light for me years ago, when I was working with an executive career coach. I had to do that for work as part of a leadership program. I remember thinking at the beginning that it was going to be too wishy-washy for me. I didn't need to delve into "feelings" – let's just all get our job done. If everyone would do their job, we wouldn't need all the mushy stuff anyway.

But that coach opened my eyes to something I'd never thought about. He came to know me as an ultra-responsible, super capable person. I could handle anything the world threw at me. And I was someone who often reached out to help others. It seemed that I was living the values I'd been raised with.

His earth-shattering question to me....

"So, how do you let others help you?" Milton asked me in a group session, with six other people waiting for my response.

I was quiet for what felt like hours. Everyone was waiting for my response to him.

"Hmmm...I guess I don't," I replied.

"When you help others and then do not allow them to help you, how do you think that makes them feel?" Milton asked.

More uncomfortable silence.

Oh...wow.... I let that sink in. LIGHT BULB moment!

I thought that probably did not feel very good to them at all. I didn't let others help me very often, and when I did, it came with great difficulty for me.

When a friend knew I was having a rough week at work and offered to help run my kids somewhere, I would refuse. When a friend offered to help me with a weekend project or with bringing food for a gathering, I would refuse. I had it *all* under control *all* of the time. I wanted to be the one who did it all. I had something to prove keeping all those balls in the air. God forbid someone grab one of my juggling balls and snatch away my superwoman glory!

Then I realized I was cutting other people off at the knees, people who only wanted to give to me.

They didn't want to help me because they thought I was incapable. They wanted a chance to give to me out of love. I was stopping them dead in their tracks.

This is when I learned one of the most valuable lessons of my life. The ability to Receive is the flip side of Generosity. Generosity without Receiving is not a full package.

If you are a generous person who gives to others and helps others, that is wonderful.

But that is only half of the story.

You have to also work on the other side - Receiving - on being open and real enough with others to allow them to give to you, on showing up as a human who also can use a hand once in a while.

Now I work on this. I try to be conscious of when others are offering help or reaching out to take something off my plate. I remind myself that receiving is another form of giving by allowing others to feel needed and important to me. When you give the appearance of not needing anyone, you are functioning only on the surface and missing half of the relationship blessings.

Allow yourself to receive. Allow yourself to be cared for. Drop your guard and be real.

Let people in to love, support, and help you even with the smallest things from errand running to helping you around the house. When others offer to help you, they are asking to love you. Let them in. That is generosity, too.

Until we can receive with an open heart, we're never really giving with an open heart. When we attach judgment to receiving help, we knowingly or unknowingly attach judgment to giving help. — Brené Brown

JOURNAL PROMPTS

Think back to the last time a friend tried to help you. What reaction did you have? What emotions did that present for you?

Identify the people in your life whom you offer generosity to and willingly help often. How many times have they attempted to reciprocate generosity back to you, and how have you responded? How do you think your reaction made them feel?

How did you respond the last time you were given a compliment?

Describe how you would graciously accept a compliment Practice accepting compliments until it becomes comfortable for you. This is a gift you can give to others as well.

Today, pay attention to each offering of help or kind comment you receive. Consciously receive each offering with love and acceptance.

DAY EIGHT

SHY, ANYONE?

I am an introvert. Those who know me well give me a puzzled look when I announce this, because they see me speak freely and without reserve. But there is a huge difference between enjoying time one on one versus in a group setting.

The definition of an introvert isn't someone who is shy or cannot socialize, rather introverts don't gain their energy from those types of interactions. For most people who consider themselves to be introverts, the opposite is true. They gain energy and are able to recharge from time spent in solitude. If you forced a few extroverts into solitude for too long, they would be more likely to create imaginary friends to socialize with instead of actually enjoying being alone. The difference isn't a matter of social skills, but on which type of interactions energize you instead of drain you.

As a child I was painfully shy, awkwardly aware that I was not comfortable speaking up in a crowd. I would rather spend an evening at home surrounded by only one or two friends than go to a party. I was the college roommate who offered to be the designated driver. I'd stay in most nights and then pick everyone up from the bars later on. I craved time alone and felt a little socially awkward because of it.

Over my life I have learned how to speak out and overcome my discomfort with strangers. I was first faced with this as a waitress paying my way through college. I quickly learned that shyness does not get you big tips! Later on, in the business world, I was thrown into the fire of public presentations. I was in my twenties and giving employee presentations about retirement to large groups. I was terrified, but I figured out how to do what I had to in order to be successful despite my discomfort.

Being skilled socially has the power to advance your career, earn you better grades and increase your popularity. But is it all at too great of a cost? Are we all pushing each other and our children to pursue the same path towards this ideal we see as success at the cost of something even more precious? What do introverts even have to offer society that extroverts cannot?

Maybe we need both types of personalities, and as a society we are misguided to place such high rewards on extroversion. Should parents train their shy children to fix their socially awkward condition, or should they instead encourage their children to engage in alone time and embrace their drive for solitude?

Do you ever feel out of place in this fast-paced, quick-talking world bustling around you?

Society teaches us to learn to speak with fluent comfortableness to others, to make small talk engaging in clever conversation at your kids' sporting events, and to communicate your ideas on teams at work – all in the interest of becoming skilled at social interaction and wooing others with your ability to connect.

Rosa Parks, Michael Jordan, Bill Gates, Abraham Lincoln, Charles Darwin, and Albert Einstein are all well known for their contributions to history – and they are all introverts. Instead of following the path of solitary practice in their craft, what if they instead had been pressured to spend time honing their conversational skills to better interact with their peers?

Who would have ever guessed that the jovial, comical, playful, imaginative, and creative Dr. Seuss was painfully shy? The same mind that could dream up all of those wondrous colorful places was uncomfortable facing his tiny, adoring fans.

Maybe those iconic people should have spent more time attending groups like Toastmasters instead of spending thousands of hours perfecting their talents. The world surely would have missed out on their brilliance. I wonder, what talents today are being undiscovered while children are guided down the standard, socially acceptable path of learning how to become something they naturally are not?

I still do not gain energy from those social interactions. Instead, they thoroughly drain me. I am exhausted after a business trip of being "on" for days. It is a sincere effort to play the part and put aside my natural tendencies. In my personal life, I crave unguided, unscheduled alone time at home to read, think, cook, or organize. I prefer to work out and run alone. Solitude is a visceral part of who I am as a human being, and if I can't find that time, I will take it unconsciously by simply shutting down when I've reached my limit of social interaction. Because of this, I pay close attention to the balance and do not starve myself of alone time.

Past people in my life have encouraged me to party more, loosen up, and engage in a lot more social activity. I recall when I was still married how deflated I'd feel to come home from a business trip – packed with days of practicing extroversion – and learn that the weekend was going to be full of social activities for me as well. Sometimes it was just too much. People who need time alone are often misunderstood as being anti-social or believed to not desire connections with others.

Fortunately, I have come to realize that what truly energizes me and brings me joy are deeper personal connections on a smaller scale, balanced with the alone time that I crave. I don't force myself to be something I am not. I don't apologize for being different.

Embrace who you were designed to be. It's the only way to feed your soul and lead an authentic life.

Everyone shines, given the right lighting. — *Susan Cain*

JOURNAL PROMPTS

Do you consider yourself to be an introvert or extrovert? How do your needs for solitude versus socialization align with the important people in your life?

For differences that do exist in your relationships, what approach do you currently use to meet your own needs while also meeting the needs of the relationship?

Are there other ways you feel out of place with the expectations of society or out of alignment with specific people in your life? How are you currently managing that feeling? What steps could you take to better manage it?

Identify a time in your life when you were called upon to be open-minded and understand someone who was different from you. Were you able to receive the differences with an open mind and heart? What would you change about your acceptance of that person or situation now?

DAY NINE

YOU WILL NEVER CATCH UP. NEVER.

I kept the second alarm clock in the bathroom. The first one was on my nightstand. The second one was a backup in case I snoozed through the first one. Hopefully, the physical act of walking from my bed to the bathroom to hit snooze would awaken me.

Nope. I would get out of bed, walk to the second alarm clock in the bathroom, hit snooze, and fall back into bed for the nine minutes more of bliss.

This was a daily occurrence. It sounds ridiculous now. I was convinced during this time of my life that less sleep was the answer to all of my problems. I would generally quit the daytime work day at three o'clock in the afternoon to make the one-hour drive back to pick up my kids. Focused "mom time" lasted from after school until eight or nine o'clock, or whenever the boys were finally asleep.

Then I would trudge back up to my home office with my first Diet Pepsi in hand to start the second shift. I'd work until midnight, falling exhausted into bed. I could fall instantly asleep despite having two and sometimes three Diet Pepsis late at night. I would set my two alarms allowing myself the reasonable four hours of sleep. I'd think to myself, *who are these people who need seven and eight hours? Sissies I say!* This was my daily routine during the week. Over the weekends I'd catch up on sleep, allowing myself six to seven hours. How generous of me. I lived on caffeine and sugar. I ate terribly. My energy was awful. My mood was cranky…but I was super productive! Or so I thought.

Eventually, I burnt out. I kept up at this pace for years. It was destructive and stupid. It damaged my health and my relationships. I put too much emphasis on work while still holding my mothering hours sacred. I justified that as long as I was one-hundred percent focused while with my boys, the rest was worth it. Thus, I scarified my sleep, my sanity, and my health.

Going through a divorce was the catalyst that finally made me change, although I wouldn't recommend that kind of catalyst. I was facing moments of huge life failure at that time, and I found it in my heart to finally quit pushing myself to unrealistic limits. Finally, I was forced to let myself fail at holding all the balls in the air, to accept the reality of it – the balls had fallen and were all at my feet for the world to see.

Then, a transformation happened. I found that it wasn't a lack of time that was my problem, but a lack of energy combined with a lack of focus. As I nursed myself through my struggles, I was good to myself for the first time in years. I slept as long as I felt that I needed. I let myself do reasonable hours at work. I did nice things for myself and focused on self-care. I started to honor my need for solitude and protected it. I healed. My priorities came into focus. My energy recovered.

Are you worried that you could be a workaholic? Do you justify it as trying to get that one next raise or promotion to put you ahead? Or maybe you're holding on for dear life at keeping the job you have, while so many people are still looking for one? Do you feel like work is sucking the life out of your very being? Maybe you want to change, and you know you should change, but you don't really know where to begin. It can be difficult once you've worked your way into certain expectations. It can feel like you can't change the rules now because people expect certain things from you and you want to meet all their expectations. You may even believe you need this for your self-esteem.

Here's the truth though: it's a vicious, never-ending cycle. The best performers are given the majority of the work. They accomplish that work because they are driven and competent. And then what happens? They are given even more work. You will never catch up.

That taunting voice that repeats over and over again – "If you just come in and work on the weekend again," or "just work nights for this week again you will finally catch up" – is lying to you.

There is no such thing as getting caught up for good. The items you cross off your list will create space for new items to be filled in. The only way to claim the time you need to be healthy and whole is to take action and set your own boundaries. Only you can set the boundaries for what you will and won't tolerate in your life and how much time you will devote to work. If you want to feel inspired, alive, and energized, you have to give yourself space to feel something, anything at all. You can't feel anything resonate if you are numb and running from place to place.

Don't get me wrong – I'm all for a great work ethic. You do have to work hard to succeed in life. There are no handouts, and teamwork is a form of loyalty lived out loud. But you need to ask yourself, *What am I working for? What is the purpose of this?* Are you working for a paycheck and superficial, empty recognition that quickly fades? Or does your work actually bring you true inner joy? And is this work the legacy you want to leave behind as your footprint?

If you're questioning whether or not you are placing too much emphasis on work and not enough on your true life joys, such as your relationships, I ask you to do one simple exercise. It may bring home a new perspective.

I am a huge believer that all the lessons we need to become the person we are destined to be are around us every day, dancing around us, practically shouting at us, *Stop and notice me! You're making this harder than it has to be!...* as we hustle around and bust our butts doing "life." All we have to do is slow down, open up, and the universe will step in to reveal what it is we need to grow, right now, right here, if we are willing to receive it.

Here is your assignment: Drive to your local airport. Park in the ramp. Leave your phone in the car. Enter the airport. Grab a cup of coffee, smoothie, soda … whatever you like. Make your way to the waiting area for unticketed passengers. The area where families wait for loved ones, where children and wives greet soldiers, where grandparents greet grandbabies, where old college friends reunite. The area of Welcome Home signs and flowers, hugs, tears, and a few squeals of sheer joy. Have a seat, and simply people-watch for however much time you have. Take your time, and let the scenes speak to you. Watch the anticipation before the reunion. Watch the faces of those waiting. Watch the emotions and hugs pour out of all these strangers around you. Watch them walk off arm-in-arm to go enjoy each other. Feel the atmosphere of raw emotion, joy, and drops in stress and anxiety. This is not just a lesson for your brain to process, but for your heart and soul to feel the weight of.

Don't just imagine this scene; give this experience to yourself. Actually do it, feel it. For an hour's worth of your time, let the world speak to you.

It's been said that someone need only to look at two items of yours to determine your true values. The first is your calendar. The second is your checking account. Do the things you say that you value show up in how you spend your time? Do the same values show up in how you spend your hard-earned money?

Think about what you wish your footprint to be here. If your last day on earth was tomorrow, what regrets would you have? Make sure you're not paying more than it's worth to you in the end, because we can't go back. I've read several articles that interview people about their dying regrets, and never once have I heard of anyone on their deathbed wishing they had spent more time at work.

What can you do differently today to set new boundaries? How can you align your daily choices more closely with the life values which you hold dear in your heart? Starting today, take a small step toward making the footprint of your life what you want it to be. Knowing it or not, you'll have worked on your life legacy today. What did you build today?

Things which matter most must never be at the mercy of things which matter least. — Johann Wolfgang von Goethe

JOURNAL PROMPTS

Do the airport exercise. Journal about what you witnessed and the emotions you felt at silently observing the reunions. What message did you take away from this exercise?

This week, track how you spend your time. Jot down each night how many hours you devoted to each area of your life. At the end of the week, review how you spent your most valuable resource. How does that resonate for you when comparing your time spent to what you hold dear?

What areas did you spend time on that don't align with your values? What activities did you say "yes" to when you felt *no* in your heart? Journal out how you will deliver your *no* next week for those activities. Practice the art of declining invitations that don't align with your goals. Protect your time as sacred. Create your legacy instead of working on someone else's.

DAY TEN

CHEESECAKE MOMENTS

My son Drew and I slide into the booth at The Cheesecake Factory, his pick for supper after we have just selected his present for his thirteenth birthday that is in a couple weeks. We are just getting settled and looking over the menus when, off to my left, I notice an elderly couple, maybe in their late seventies. They are enjoying what looks to be after-dinner coffee drinks.

I find old couples fascinating, and I watch this couple intently. I wonder...*have they been together fifty years? Is this one of thousands of meals they have shared, or did they find each other late in life?* They are quietly enjoying their conversation. They look content and accepting of each other, not jovial or putting on airs. They don't really appear to be making an effort at conversation. They just look to be comfortable being together and enjoying each other's company in a very simple, beautiful way.

I point them out to my son. "Oh...!" he exclaims. "I looove old people!" This makes me smile. I watch him watching them and can tell he has the same reaction, one of admiration and joy that tiny, happy moments exist at all stages of life.

Suddenly the server interrupts our view and sets down in front of the elderly couple two enormous, full-size pieces of cheesecake. My son and I exchange huge grins at the same time, just how cute and wonderful it is to witness this simple joy.

My son returns to looking at the box of his new birthday present, mesmerized by the prospects of his new tech toy. I am still thinking about the old couple with a smile and noticing the acoustical music playing in the background, the sound of clanking silverware, and the servers all bustling around us dressed in white.

Then I notice another booth to the right, behind the older couple. A brand new family with a tiny baby is sitting there. The dad is trying to be as gentle as possible to get this small, squirming bundle of flesh into his car-seat carrier. The new mom, possibly still donning maternity attire, looks on at her husband. She looks worn out. I wonder if this is one of their first outings as a new family. My heart tugs. I remember those days, the unsure feeling every new day brings as you make your way through the new-parent maze with this incredible gift now in your constant care.

My vision now switches to my son sitting across from me, and it hits me like a sledge hammer: We are not here at the start any longer; we are not yet at the end, though. Here we sit, smack dab in the middle of the circle of life. I am about halfway through my circle. I feel the weight of that realization settle in deep as I can still see both families in my vision, reminding me to savor this moment, enjoy the journey, and love each step along the way.

I view the whole scene, lost in my thoughts on how beautiful the circle of life is all laid out before me in these touching visuals during a random restaurant meal. I wonder how many other visual messages I have missed that have before been laid out before me, because I was too busy to see them. I promise myself to slow down and notice more, feel more, listen more to the moments.

We all know our time here is limited and unknown, but somehow we still manage to ignore that truth as we speed through our days. Mortality is a topic most of us won't discuss or think about, but we each feel its weight. When we're in our twenties, the weight is nonexistent. We still have our whole lives ahead of us. In our thirties, we are aware of the time passing but can be so busy with obligations that we still don't feel it. Then, suddenly in our forties, it's like we emerge from a coma. We look around us and are shocked that the movie reel of our life is perhaps halfway over. Urgency and panic can strike us as we come to grips with our temporary nature. It's an impossible concept to swallow all at once. If you take this truth in as small daily bites, it can settle into your soul and change the way you live.

Every day remind yourself that this day is a gift. *I will never have another like it. No matter what the day brings, let me find joy within the moments and lessons around me. Let me move slowly enough to notice what is here for me. Let me be thankful and willing to enjoy the experience of simply being alive.* It is quite a miracle that any of us is even here at all. Instead of trying to control life and making it fit our good or bad definition based on our desires, what if we let it be an experience that washes over us daily? A beautiful miracle that we are blessed to experience every day.

My son asks at the end of dinner, "Cheesecake tonight, Mom?"

My response of course is, "Absolutely, honey!"

I hope you'll slow down. I hope you'll open yourself to let the moments speak to you and touch you. And I hope you'll always savor the cheesecake moments.

Life is defined by time, appreciate the beauty of time. — Lailah Gifty Akita

JOURNAL PROMPTS

Reflect on the speed of your life. How urgent are you feeling about the time passing in your journey? How do your feelings today compare to those of five years ago? Ten years ago?

Are you on path, on track to fully value each day, or do you need to steer with a drastic turn to make a change and get on course?

What daily action will you put in place to create a habit that allows you to savor the moments? It could be a morning journal or an evening gratitude practice. It could be some quiet prayer or meditation time. Choose one small new habit to implement this week and journal about how that affected you.

DAY ELEVEN

THREE GENERATIONS – RUNNING

STRONG

As I left my son just before we reached the race finish line, I fist-bumped him, flashed a beaming smile, and did a one-eighty turn to start running in the opposite direction from the finish line.

In my day it would have been a high-five, but apparently now it's all in the fist bump. As I started running back against the flow of the runners coming at me, I saw anxious looks on their faces, as if they were asking, "How much farther? Will I make it?" I shouted a "Good job! Keep it up!" to each one. The crowd running against me became thinner, but the faces seemed much more desperate. I was looking for my dad.

My thoughts were suddenly flooded with snippets from the past. Every day of childhood I woke up to a list, written in my dad's barely legible handwriting, that would include several cleaning chores, extra school work, and always – without fail – a significant amount of physical activities, often running. Nothing was allowed before the list was completed – no TV, no friends, no phone. You earned your freedom each and every day.

I started running with dad when I was very young, and I remember him signing me up without my knowledge or agreement for a 10K race when I was only about ten years old. I think I was the last runner to complete that race, and I remember crying and cursing my dad for making me do that awful horrendous thing that I clearly thought was too much to ask of a ten-year-old.

There I was thirty-some years later, having dropped off my son at the finish line and going back to find my dad and run to the end with him. When he signed up for this, Dad was adamant that, "No one runs pace with me, you each run your own race." It had been several years since dad and I ran a race together.

The last one we tried was painful for him. He struggled much more than he anticipated after his double-heart bypass and was not happy to see his body fail to rise to the occasion. For years now he has only walked. He walks religiously to keep his diabetes in check and keep up with his goal of no insulin. But when my son Drew started taking up running, my dad had a new reason to rediscover the activity – the opportunity to run with his grandson.

I saw him then off in the distance. It brought a heavy ache to my heart to see him older, grayer, and frailer than I liked to admit. But, there he was trudging away, putting one foot in front of the other at a slow jog. I thought back to the days when he was the one pushing me, telling me not to stop and that I could do it. I remembered when his calves were the topic of conversation among my friends, who were always in awe of how strong he looked. His thighs were each about as big around as my entire waist. Time is truly a thief of our bodies, for sure, even if not of our souls.

He smiled at me and I turned to be by his side. We exchanged high fives and his first words were, "How did Drew do?" My heart was filled with an overwhelming sense of gratitude for that very moment. My dad and I had never had the kind of relationship where you really talked about intimate life details. Instead he had showed me through his commitment and actions how to stick things out in life. He had showed me how to never give up no matter how hard things are.

Over the years I cursed those daily lists, cursed having to run, even cursed him, but in that moment, seeing him as human and vulnerable as he was, I realized something. We were both leaning on each other and leading each other at the same time through this life. My dad's beaming smile at the finish line said it all, and I am simply thankful for that moment.

Running is about finding your inner peace, and so is a life well lived.

— *Dean Karnazes*

JOURNAL PROMPTS

Take a few moments to dig up old photos of your family members. As you look at each picture, journal the feelings that come up while looking at the snippets of the past. What does your heart feel when you examine each picture? Can you remember what you were going through in your life when each picture was taken?

How has your life changed since then, and, more importantly, how has your perspective on these relationships changed? We are all growing through our life journeys, on separate paths that intertwine with those surrounding us. How has your relationship changed since these pictures were taken?

Do you have any special moments or traditions in your life that connect generations together, such as running has for me in this story? Life is marching right by. Our goal isn't to cling or hang on, but to fully immerse our souls in the experience of today while still honoring the value of all of our life experiences. Traditions help us do both at the same time. Value the present while honoring the past. What else can you do to foster connection through shared experiences?

DAY TWELVE

WE CHOOSE OUR JOURNEY HERE

One day I explained to my son, who was three at the time, that someday he will probably find a girl that he really likes, fall in love with her, and then marry her. He will spend the rest of his life with her.

He replies, "I already know who I am going to marry, Mom."

I ask him, "Who?" expecting he will tell me about a girl from his preschool class.

"You, Mom," he replies. "I want to marry you."

My heart stops for a moment at how tenderly sweet this moment is. Right now, I am the woman of his dreams. I am the most beautiful woman to this three-year-old boy. I am the prettiest and nicest girl he has ever known. He loves to touch my hair and loves to kiss me goodnight. He tells me he loves me about ten times a day, just out of the blue. He loves to share secrets with me and knows that I'll laugh at all of his corny jokes.

He knows that I will be here for him forever and will always take care of him. He trusts me to protect him from anything that may ever hurt him. He knows that even if I get angry with him, I still love him more than anything in this world. Right now, at this time for him, I am the true love of his life.

And I suddenly realize that twenty-some years from now, he really will meet someone whom he will fall deeply in love with. I think for a moment how that will feel to witness. I will have to find a way to gracefully step down as the first woman of his dreams and hand him over to the woman he chooses. He will no longer look at me as the most beautiful, funniest woman in the room, as the woman whose hugs and kisses are better than candy. He will no longer share all his secrets with me. And, by that time, he will realize that I will not be here forever. And try as I might, I cannot protect him from all that is wrong in this world.

The transition from "love of his life" to" mother of the groom" will of course be gradual, but will happen much too fast for me. The next twenty-some years will turn my little boy into a man. It will be a transition of great joy and great pain for both of us, stretching the limits of our bonds so tightly that we may barely be hanging on. There will be times that he will say he hates me, and I know he will genuinely feel every word of it at the time.

Somehow in the next twenty-some years I have to figure out how to let go with grace and not feel like my heart is leaving my body when he leaves the house. I have no idea how to get to the other side, and I frankly have no desire to get there. It's a journey we signed on for together, though, and I owe it to him to live out my end of that journey with the most grace possible. I believe we choose our parents and that our kids choose us to some degree. I imagine it to be like some kind of consultation on our assignment with God.

"Here's what I have planned for you," God might say to the child soul. As he explains the journey required, lessons to be learned, and role to play, the soul creates the intention with Him to do His work.

This may be an odd or even sacrilegious belief to some people, but it was an idea that helped me tremendously when I had a devastating pregnancy loss before either of my boys.

We had waited until age thirty to try for a family, and being the controlling planner that I am, I scheduled for us to achieve pregnancy in two months of trying and we would produce a baby in May of 2000. When I discovered the first month that I wasn't pregnant, I was fine with that. The second month, I was late. I fully believed my plan had worked. But when I had my period nearly ten days late, I knew that even if I had been pregnant, I no longer was.

Something didn't feel right to me, and a few days later I took a pregnancy test. I don't know why. Nothing told me I was still pregnant except a nagging feeling that something wasn't right. When the test result showed up as a full bright line, positive happiness is not what I felt. Fear is all I felt. I knew based on the cycle I had just had, no baby could have survived.

I called the doctor the next day, a Monday. He wanted me to come in for a blood test to figure out what was going on. He thought I'd most likely miscarried and still had the pregnancy hormone in my body to explain for the positive test.

I had the test and he called the nest day with the results. My hormone levels were right on track and perfect for someone five weeks pregnant.

"What?" I asked.

"Now we need to see if the levels are doubling like they should be. Come back in tomorrow for another test."

I tried not to let my heart soar. I tried not to feel a connection with the life I hoped was growing inside me. I told myself to not commit to a feeling until I knew more. I tried to not root for the impossible.

I went in for the blood test the next day and they called me back that afternoon. The doctor called. Apparently, this was a special case.

"Your levels doubled," he said. "That means it appears you have a viable pregnancy."

"What?! I am pregnant?" After all of that, somehow, I was still pregnant? My heart soared as I thought about my amazing little miracle baby who was a fighter before I even knew she existed. I don't know why, but it was a girl to me. I guess because of the strength.

I had to keep going in for blood tests every two days. As long as my levels doubled every two days, all was fine and we would do an ultrasound at eight to ten weeks to listen for the heartbeat. We were on our way! And what a special start she and I had together.

I continued going and the hCG hormone levels kept doubling.

Until. They weren't.

At what would have been about eight weeks, they stopped doubling. My heart plummeted as deep down as it had soared high.

"Come back in two days and let's check it again," the doctor said.

Two days? That was like a year to me. Fortunately, I was busy. I was working on my MBA and had projects due to put my focus on. The next day after work when I was getting ready for class, I started to have cramping. These were not just mild cycle cramps, but cramps so deep that I couldn't stand up straight. I was doubled over in pain and just before I was scheduled to leave for class, I realized how ridiculous I was thinking that I could still go. I couldn't even stand up.

I went to bed, curled in a ball on my side, and waited. I waited for the bleeding to start, waited to see the truth that my baby wasn't going to make it. I envisioned how horrible it was going to be.

But nothing else really happened. I called my doctor in the morning to tell him, and he wanted me to get up to the hospital immediately for an ultrasound. The goal was to see if we could tell what was going on.

I drank an ocean of water and held my bladder until it stretched to the size of a hot air balloon, finally making it through the internal ultrasound.

My doctor called me that night. "I'd like you to meet me at the hospital tomorrow at five a.m. for surgery. I believe you have a tubal or ectopic pregnancy."

He explained that while he couldn't see a mass on the ultrasound, my symptoms all led to that conclusion. The pain was due to the fetus pushing on my fallopian tube where he believed the baby was stuck. A baby can't grow anywhere but in your uterus. The baby was destined to terminate. The main goal was to maintain my health and prevent eruption and serious internal bleeding. I wasn't to move around much or eat much for dinner, just drink liquids and nothing at all after midnight.

I spent the night thinking about my child who never would be. I thought about whether or not I should believe the doctor's recommendation. What if my little girl could still be a miracle? I was basically being asked to abort my child, give up on my child. I was the mom. I was supposed to give my life to protect her, but instead I was going to kill her to protect myself. What did that make me?

We met the doctor at the hospital and he wanted to try a nonsurgical procedure. It involved injecting me with a chemotherapy drug called methotrexate. The drug would seek out any abnormally multiplying, fast-growing cells and destroy them. In other words, it would seek out my baby and destroy it. He explained that if I didn't do this, the result would most likely be an eruption of my fallopian tube with internal bleeding and emergency surgery. I'd most likely lose at least one of my tubes and up to fifty percent of my chances for a future viable pregnancy.

I took the drug. I accepted a chemical I knew would kill my baby. I'd never felt more despair in my life. After the procedure, we had to attend some family events. I was zoned out and just getting through the day. We didn't tell anyone we'd been trying, so I didn't want to share my pain. I was silent.

The silence grew into nearly two months of depression. I'd never been depressed in my life. I felt so much guilt. I knew in my logical brain that making a decision other than what I did, would have risked my own life. But my heart felt like I'd forsaken my daughter. I felt like a failure as a mother before I even was one.

I'd been raised Catholic and had very black and white views about abortion. To me, it was always wrong. It was wrong in rape. It was wrong in incest. It was always against God. The only way was to let nature take its course and let God decide. But that was not what I did. Was God trying to teach me a lesson? Bring me as close as he could to coming face-to-face with my own judgement to teach me something? If I was going to make leeway for myself to end a life, maybe I had to make more leeway than I had been for other situations that I knew nothing of.

I still believed abortion is wrong, yet I had aborted in a sense to save my own life. What did that mean? All I could come to is that God was trying to point out to me my own self-righteous nature and that not everything is as it seems. Most people would say equating the necessary procedure I'd been forced to do as abortion was ludicrous. But that doesn't change how it felt to me in my heart.

During my depression, I recall seeing a TV interview on Oprah with a couple that had just lost their baby hours after he was born. The grief counselor said, "Don't you see….your son picked you. Your son knew he was signing up for the shortest journey possible with you. He knew it would be painful. He knew he wouldn't make it, and yet he still chose you. He signed up for this brief, beautiful interaction with your souls and his, knowing full well the sacrifice. He loves you that much."

Being raised Catholic, this sounded crazy to me, and yet I grasped onto that idea with all that I had. What if she had chosen me, knowing the brevity of it? What if she had said to God, "Yes, I will serve this role for you and help you show her love."

Ever since then I've believed that we pick our journeys before we are born. I know it's not accepted by some religions. But if God is in us and God is in nature and God is in the world and we are all inter-connected, who's to say we didn't start this journey together in collective agreement?

Instead of viewing God as the all-knowing controller, I think of Him as an integrated part of me that is co-creating this journey. He asked me if I would serve this role and I agreed. I still agree. Every day I ask him to speak to me and guide me and remember what I am called here for. It is a partnership, not a dictatorship. If I have a role now in carrying out His work, why is it crazy to believe I had a role before my physical birth?

This belief changed the way I see many things in the world. For example, when I see a disabled person who was born with challenging physical or mental disabilities, I don't feel pity. I don't feel sorry for them or wish that their situation was different. I only feel great reverence and honor at the gift they have chosen to give us. I find myself completely humbled by their strength and love.

I believe they agreed to this path with God to help teach others what we can only learn through someone with their special combination of gifts and challenges. I feel humbled at being in the presence of such a strong and advanced soul that they were capable of taking on the most challenging of journeys possible. That doesn't excuse me from feeling for them; it changes the type of feeling I have for them from one of pity and helplessness to one of reverent respect for their intention here. I feel a fluid openness to what they came here to teach me.

While our journeys may be painful and difficult at times, I believe I signed up for this journey with my children. It's part of my duties to carry out my role with grace to the best of my ability.

Meanwhile I will continue to hold on to all those little-boy kisses and hugs as long as I possibly can. For now, I will enjoy the honor of being the first true love of this little three-year-old boy's life. Later I will enjoy watching him create his own journey and live out his plan with God as I embrace my new role in his life.

There's nowhere you can be that isn't where you're meant to be..." — John Lennon

JOURNAL PROMPTS

How does the idea of having chosen this journey sit with you? Can you identify in your life some common themes among your struggles that make you wonder if those hold the key to your purpose here?

How do you envision God working in your life? Is He in charge and control, or is He there to lead and guide? Do you believe there is a plan already determined for your life or that you are in control of what happens in your life?

What areas of your own spiritual or religious path have you struggled with? Have you been raised or educated in certain beliefs that no longer ring true for you? What beliefs have you developed on your own that differ from your upbringing and how authentic are you in expressing your own beliefs?

DAY THIRTEEN

ARE YOU WILLING TO GIVE UP WHAT YOU HAVE FOR WHAT YOU WANT?

This question, if you can answer it, solves nearly all of life's dilemmas that most of us struggle with and spend energy on daily. It seems like a simple enough question, but clearly it is not.

People struggle with relationships that they feel are less than they deserve. They wonder if there is something better for them out there. There might be, but are you willing to give up what you have right now, today? That is a tough leap for many of us to make. Or, maybe you need to give up some of your own personal tendencies or limiting beliefs to make the relationship you are in a better one? What stories do you tell yourself that you turn into a self-fulfilling prophecy?

Many of us also struggle with fitness and health. We want to be healthy, we want to exercise, we plan to eat right, but the couch draws us in and the convenience food is, well, all so convenient and yummy! Are you willing to give up some TV shows and couch time for what you want? Are you willing to spend a bit more time preparing your food to get what you want? Willing to give up the sugary treats and fried foods? Maybe you often explore the idea of trying something new and then say, "I could never do that. I could never prep all my food on Sunday. I could never pack my lunch each day."

Our jobs also pose the same question. If you are not happy in your current job, are you willing to give that up for following your passion and dream of what you really want? If you are not willing to make a full swap exchange at that chance, then are you willing to invest some of your current free time towards following your dream? What are you willing to give up for what you want?

Do you want to live closer to loved ones so that you can see them more and share more of your lives together? Maybe you want to be there to be a caregiver for your parents. What are you willing to give up to make these things happen? Are you willing to move your family, change jobs and homes, and live where they are? If you simply want to move to a nicer climate, the same questions apply.

Do you wish you had more time to read books, travel more, or work on your hobby? What are you willing to give up in exchange to make those things happen?

We must do something different to achieve something different, and frankly most of us don't want to. We say we want to, but our actions say otherwise.

And here is the tough-love part, friends. If you've been saying that any of these things are things you've been wanting for years and have yet to find it within yourself to make any significant changes, I'd argue that you don't really want what you say you want... at least not right now or you would have made it happen by now.

If you are not willing to give up what you have to get what you say you want, then you need to stop being negative about what you have and instead be thankful for it. After all, you chose it. Yes, this life didn't just happen to you. You chose it. And by "chose it" I mean pretty much all of it. No, you can't choose all of the events that happen to you, but we all know that life is not so much what happens to you as much as it is what you do with it.

How many terminal cancer patients have drastically changed the world and inspired thousands of people in how they chose to live a beautiful life? There are hundreds of inspirations built out of horrible circumstances. Don't you dare use what has happened to you as an excuse. You chose where you are.

Stop spreading negativity and complaining to those around you about your relationship, the cold winters, the humid summers, how much you hate your job, or the current status of your health or finances.

It is often simply a choice you've actually made. No one is forcing you to keep what you have now as being part of your future. At any time, you can change your mind and give up what you have in exchange for what you really want. But only you can make that decision if the benefit outweighs the cost, and only you are responsible for making that choice. There is no one else to blame or to celebrate for where you are in your life journey. Do you find that to be empowering or limiting? I guess that is all up to you!

Please read that last paragraph again – you can change your mind at any time. You can even change right now, this instant. There's no need to wait for tomorrow or Monday or next January First. If you don't like what you picked and where it landed, you start over. It's that simple. It's not complicated at all.

Set your intentions about what you want. Decide on the steps necessary to set yourself in that direction and take that first step. Then take the next step, and so on. I assure you that you'll land somewhere different and closer to your desired outcome. Living with intention is a daily practice. Tune in with your desires and set yourself in motion to move towards them. Simple it is. Easy it's not.

You will stand in your own way. Fear will join in the fight. But what do you really want? Are you willing to go get it? If your answer is yes, then push through all that will pop up in your way. Keep saying yes until you get there. You're so worth it.

To say you have no choice is to relieve yourself of responsibility. — *Patrick Ness*

JOURNAL PROMPTS

Think back to the dreams you had for life as a young adult. How many of your dreams are part of your life now? Why or why not?

If you found out you had only three months to live, what changes would you make first and why?

Identify one dream that your words keep committing to but your actions do not. Explore below if you will let go of that dream or commit yourself to it more deeply with new action. What action will you take this week to set that in motion?

DAY FOURTEEN

HOPE FOR MY BOYS

I wake up and look around. I love my home, but I wish sometimes for less space filled with less stuff. When did I lose interest in nearly everything we are told to work towards as young adults?

As I watch my boys grow up, as any mom, I have so many hopes and dreams for them. I am finding that my stage in life is causing me to reflect more deeply on what message I really send my boys on a daily basis.

As we lead our kids through the structure and rules of life, how do we encourage them to have vibrant imaginations and follow their passions to feed their souls at the same time?

In one breath, I find myself encouraging them to strive for high GPAs, but at the same I'm time worried they will avoid taking risks towards true growth in their lives. I worry about our schools causing conformity and killing our kids' dreams. I worry that our busy lives and mortgaged homes will lead them down a path that stifles their future to be in the same status quo. We want our kids to do well in school, get great grades, be well-liked, go to college, and get a job that brings them success. We want them to buy homes and pay mortgages just like us. That is American success after all.

But how many of us followed that path for decades? And then how many of us at midlife take a break to look around at the lives we have made, and find that much of what we once sought is now a little empty? Many of us ask ourselves what it was all for.

Why, then, do we lead our children down this same path? Is it even possible to reach your own enlightenment for your path without first getting lost?

These answers elude me and change day to day for me. Hard work, responsibility, and good character are all traits I encourage my kids to resemble, because I know these traits will bring them success in the form of some stability and self-reliance. At the same time, I try to discourage perfectionism and conformity. I point out that we should not merely accept what society shoves at us to be as desirable as our true inner desires. The idea that body image, relationship status, and material wealth is the end-all reward from success is just an empty vessel.

What I do tell my boys is that while all these rules and structures and societal successes grant you some stability, they can also stifle your spirit. They can cause conformity if you aren't careful to nurture and listen to your soul.

I ask them often, "If money were no concern, and you had to leave the house to do something each day, what would that be?" Or, "If you could pick anything in the entire world to be doing today, what would it be?"

I know that as their mom, my job is to prepare them for this world by teaching them to become self-sufficient and employable among other things. But I also feel a great responsibility to show them that there is more to life than fitting into this society. We aren't here to just follow a career path. We need to listen to and follow our soul path. How do I guide them not only through the years, but through to the end in a way that they have as few regrets as possible?

I feel grateful for the solid foundation I was given in that it has enabled me to become successful and stable enough to even have thoughts surrounding whether my soul path is on track. I know that living and providing comes before dreaming. It's hard to imagine my grandmother worrying about things like what her life's passion and soul purpose was beyond feeding and providing for her family. But I also know that meaningless success melts faster than wedding cake frosting on your tongue.

I hope that I can inspire my boys to awaken to their true purposes before they reach their halfway points in life. My hope is that they can find that path that meets both life's necessity of living and their soul's necessity of reaching their destiny.

We must march on with love, doing the best we can and hoping for the next generation to take a crack at this journey in an even more noble attempt than we have.

The purpose of life is a life of purpose. — Robert Bryne

JOURNAL PROMPTS

Do you have a repeated wish for your life or a goal you are putting off until the time is right?

How do you balance creating a life of meaning and substance with one of necessity? How do you make time for your soul calling while making a living?

Have you had any changes over your life in your goals? What milestones were once crucial to your definition of success you now question as relevant for your life?

Identify someone in your life whom you feel exemplifies this balance of life purpose with daily necessities. Reach out and ask for their philosophy on how they achieve this balance.

DAY FIFTEEN

LESSONS ON AGING

The tough part about growing older has nothing to do with my face falling in the general direction of my chin and jawline. The tough part isn't the wrinkles or the age spots that show my days blessed by the sun. It's not even the clear fact that I am no longer noticed. I rather like fading into the scenery in public places.

The tough part for me has to do with letting go. This is especially true with my boys as I feel them release their needs of me and make their ways out into this wondrous world. I watch with pride, mixed with fear and even a tinge of envy for their wide-eyed welcome to whatever they can discover. They are open to it all with abandon.

As I reach new milestones of natural detachment and try to embrace my own new life phase, I often think of my own parents. I now know what they went through. I know the gift they gave to me by letting go of me and allowing me to find my way. I can look at them now with a new-found appreciation, understanding, and a touch of sadness to know how I made them feel. These feelings of their pain were as oblivious to me at the time as they are to my boys right now, as it should be.

At the same time, I watch my boys with wonder and awe. I envy the days that you welcomed the instability of life, that you yearned for changes that even caused the ground beneath you to seem to shift, and to find that to be exciting instead of fearful.

Aging brings such enlightenment as well as pains when it takes so long to see certain truths and realize how long the process of understanding takes us as humans.

As you experience more of life, you realize how much is out of your control. You realize how little your plans mean to the actual final outcome. Fear starts to overtake excitement after living long enough to witness the pain of existing. A long life guarantees that you will wrestle against some very painful life events. You start to understand in the fiber of your being that God is steering the car. Before you knew the words and concept, but by now you have let that truth settle more fully into your being.

Aging brings a weightiness to life that we must delve into so that we appreciate it all and soak it in before time runs out. I know this, and yet I long for the light free-footed feeling of welcoming the ground to shift beneath me again instead of spending my days trying to steady my footing.

These lessons have taught me to learn and enjoy both acts of looking ahead of me and behind me. All the pieces of life stick messily together to create the version of me that I am today.

Yes, even when face-falling down towards the ground and all, I know that each day to learn more in this life is a gift I am privileged to hold.

There is a fountain of youth: it is your mind, your talents, the creativity you bring to your life and the lives of people you love. When you learn to tap this source, you will truly have defeated age. — Sophia Loren

JOURNAL PROMPTS

On a scale of one to ten, how comfortable are you with your aging?

What do you want to experience in life that you have not yet?

Can you think of an older person who seems much younger due to their spirit alone? How are they different than other people you know?

Begin a bucket list of experiences, accomplishments, or conversations you want to have yet in your life. I challenge you to come up with a list of one hundred items you want to experience before you leave this place. It's a lot harder than it sounds and it is a great exercise to get back in touch with your dreams.

DAY SIXTEEN

WHY WE NEED FAILURES

I was thirteen. I had learned how to drive a car that summer. Manual transmission/stick shift of course. Automatic was a luxury and for sissies. So, I knew how to drive, barely. It was the first snowfall of the winter. Dad grabbed the keys and said, "Let's go. You need to learn how to drive on snow."

"What?" I hardly knew how to drive without lurching the car forward. And who could forget the afternoon I backed up traffic on the hill? I was still getting the hang of the clutch release and close to twenty cars lined up behind me as I proceeded to kill the engine over and over again, stalling repeatedly. The pressure was intense and so embarrassing for a teenager. But, you didn't get to tell my dad no.

I was so nervous. Our gravel driveway was long and lined by a fence that divided our drive from the neighbors. We lived out in the country on a gravel road next to a farmstead. Our house was not a farm, and neither were the other few houses on the road. We just lived next to one.

Dad got me going by saying, "Just drive like you normally would, only a bit slower."

"Okay. Sure." The snow was sparkling silver underneath the headlight path. The wheels spun on the freshly laid snow. I could feel the car slipping and sliding, so I gave it more gas to get her going.

Took off we did! We shot right out of the driveway, fishtailing and sliding. Bam! I shot myself right into the ditch on the other side of our road, just missing a telephone pole and nearly crashing the family car I knew my parents could barely afford. The only good thing I could see was that at least I had not hit the pole. I couldn't imagine much worse an outcome than the one I had just produced.

Dad got out of the car and told me to get out. I could tell he was frustrated and doubting this exercise in faith. He went to the neighbor's farm to ask him to pull us out with his tractor. I went inside the house to try to stay out of the way and tend to my wounded pride. I watched them work, looking out the front window. Mom didn't say much other than, "It'll be okay, honey." I could tell though that it was a worry to them both as to whether the car would need any work.

After the tractor pulled the car out, Dad parked it back in the drive and came inside.

Then, something amazing happened. Dad said, "Come on, let's go. Car's running. You need to get back in there and try it again."

"What? Now? You want me to drive now, after I just landed my first try in the ditch twenty yards away?"

"Yep. You have to get back in there and do it or you will hold onto your fear. You must do it right now. No waiting."

God, was I nervous, even more nervous than the first time. But I felt something else, too. Determination. Courage. And I felt the faith my dad had in me that I could do it. If he believed in me, maybe I could, too. *How could he believe in me when I had failed so big?*

I didn't know then that it was a life lesson in the making, but now I do. I've been thinking of that moment recently as I've been reflecting on the role confidence plays in our success in life.

As girls and women, we do not have the same levels of confidence as men generally do. This is for many reasons – societal upbringing, social norms, brain biology, hormones. The lack of confidence, although it is real, is one-hundred percent unfounded. Women are as competent as men and in some situations even more competent. A lack of confidence does not in any way equate to a lack of competence. We tend to stand in our own way because of pure fabricated storytelling and fear.

Closely related to the theme of confidence and how we obtain confidence is failure and how we view it. Think of Confidence as one side of the coin with Failure as the backside. Confidence shows up more easily when failure is seen as a possibility.

Perfection is brick wall to confidence. If we wait to move forward until we're perfect, we will never take action. But when we embrace failure as a learning tool instead of the end of the line, our confidence is compelled to show up.

If we fail and don't pick ourselves up off the floor to go after it again, or dig ourselves out of the snowy ditch to take off again, then yes failure is the end of the line. But when we view failure as a necessary step towards learning and growth, we can show up as more authentic and genuine in who we are. We can grow our abilities and show confidence that no matter how many missteps we take, we will eventually achieve what we came here to do.

If I can give only one piece of advice to young women and girls it is to face your fear and do it anyway. *Fail fast. Fail often. Fail brave.* See failure as your fastest path to lasting success. Do not wait until you are feeling one-hundred percent ready. You will never feel ready. Do prepare, yes, but then dig in and go for it. Take risks. And when you fall down, get back up with more determination and courage, and resolve than before.

Repeat as often as necessary. Confidence comes with trust in yourself. Trust that you can handle anything that comes your way, because you've already broken through all the walls you had falsely constructed for yourself.

I've failed many times in my life. My biggest failures were absolutely my most efficient teachers. I can look back now and feel gratitude for each and every lesson no matter how painful they were at the time.

I guess Dad knew what he was doing all along.

There is only one thing that makes a dream impossible to achieve: the fear of failure. — Paulo Coelho, The Alchemist

120

JOURNAL PROMPTS

How confident are you on a scale of one to ten? You can examine this question in different areas – parenting, career, relationships. Describe your rating and reasons in each area.

Identify your biggest failure in life so far. What effect did that event have on your self-worth at the time you were going through the experience? Looking back now, how have you absorbed that experience into your being? Do your feelings surrounding that failure differ now with the added perspective of time?

Identify one thing you want to try, but the thought of failure has held you back. Commit to one step in the direction of what you want. How can you move into it knowing that failure is acceptable as a stepping stone on your path?

DAY SEVENTEEN

PLAYING SMALL ISN'T NICE

One of the biggest women's issues today is the wage gap, the opportunity gap. It's real and the numbers don't lie.

Women, on average, earn less than men in virtually every single occupation for which there is sufficient earnings data for both men and women to calculate an earnings ratio. Most studies place the gap at about 20%, and it's significantly worse for minorities.

We want equal pay, responsibilities, and advancement opportunities. Even if you are a woman who doesn't choose a career outside the home right now for yourself, you surely want your daughters and nieces to have better opportunities.

Maybe we as women need to review the small signals we send the world, the ones that say we are willing to play small so as not to upset anyone or make anyone uncomfortable.

How many times has a person next to you on an airplane taken up the entire arm rest and spread their legs wide into your space? As you folded your arms into your body and touched your own knees together to shrink the space you were taking up, what thoughts ran through your head? Did you say something? What about your comfort? Did it matter enough to make yourself uncomfortable in speaking up? Or was it okay to trade your discomfort to avoid the confrontation?

What is it about being a woman that makes us more likely to sacrifice our comfort at the expense of others, even when unwarranted?

There are many opposing articles on female communication styles and how we use a lot of speech qualifiers that weaken our message. The following words are a few examples:

- Just
- I feel, I believe, or I think
- I'm not really sure, but...
- I may be wrong, but...
- Right?
- Am I making sense? Do I make sense?
- What if we maybe tried this...
- Sorry. Sorry. Oh, did I mention I'm sorry.

The list is endless. We do use these words more than men. There's even an app for it. Gmail has a tool you can use to check your emails for this softening language that weakens your message delivery. It's called Just Not Sorry.

If you believe this communication style enhances your message, then I say go for it. But it's at least worth reflecting on and asking yourself why you use these softeners. Is the purpose to make someone else feel more comfortable? Do you tiptoe into your own strength and purpose instead of shining in them brightly like the beacon that you are?

Plus, who are you to decide that what others want is for you to soften your message on their behalf?

We keep saying that we want a different future. Maybe we need to do things differently, even small ways. I'm not asking women to act like men or mimic anyone else's communication style. As women, we owe it to ourselves not to suffer our own discomfort solely because we don't want our light to shine too brightly in anyone else's eyes.

Playing small doesn't only hurt women. It hurts everyone. There are brilliant minds with world-changing ideas floating around our planet, but these people are wasting time worrying about how to best float their ideas in the next meeting so they can be received as nonthreatening as necessary.

The next time sucking it up and playing small crosses your mind, I ask you to choose bigger for yourself, for women, and for our world. Even if it's asking the passenger next to you to respect your space, for starters, or speaking up boldly at the meeting without apologizing first. Small consistent changes over time can lead to huge results.

Playing small and constantly forfeiting our own needs solely to avoid discomfort or confrontation is like playing baseball from the outfield only.

Show up. Be fully present and embrace what you offer without apologies. The world is counting on you to shine your light full wattage while you are here. Your shine will encourage others to share their shine and the entire world will benefit.

In the future, there will be no female leaders. There will just be leaders.
— Sheryl Sandberg

JOURNAL PROMPTS

Light is mentioned in the bible four-hundred forty times. We are taught in the book of Matthew 5:16, "Let your light shine before men in such a way that they may see your good works, and glorify your Father who is in heaven." In what ways do you feel self-conscious when it comes to showing your talents boldly?

In what ways do you downplay your strengths to make others more comfortable around you? Why? What feelings arise in you before you take this action?

What advice do you have for young girls that is different than what you chose to follow for yourself? How can you help pave a path for future women based on what you've learned?

If you are not a woman answer these questions for what you view other women in your life doing and how you would advise them differently.

DAY EIGHTEEN

LOVE LIKE A CHILD

A nd now these three remain: faith, hope and love. But the greatest of these is love. *~1 Corinthians 13:13*

Children just know how to love. They are born knowing how to love without fear, without the need for reciprocation or rules. It is the most beautiful, truest form of real love I have ever witnessed. We have a lot to relearn as adults. Here are seven beautiful lessons we can learn from the children in our lives.

1) **Beauty.** My boys tell me I am beautiful at the most unexpected moments, and I actually believe them. I believe almost no one else who says these words to me. Why is it so easy to believe them? Because they tell me when I am feeling ugly, when I am unshowered, and looking my worst. They don't only say it when I have spent hours trying to put my best self together as a mini-project. They say it when they feel it from inside their hearts. I can tell it's more than just a comment on how I appear physically. It is something they feel about me. Ethan, my youngest is hanging out in

the home gym...literally..."hanging" on top of a piece of gym equipment, watching me walk on the treadmill. He looks at me and says, "You are so beautiful mom." My heart turns instantly into liquid joy as I say a silent prayer that he will always remember me this way.

2) **Peace.** They tell me to breathe. When I get stressed out and nutty because the house is a mess and the kids refuse to pick up after themselves, Drew, my oldest son takes a deep breath, makes this floating hand gesture to his sides, and tells me, "Just breathe, Mom, just breathe." Somehow this reminds me that the mess is not even a speck on the lens of this picture called life. I am reminded instantly to reach out instead for the connections.

3) **Acceptance.** They go with the flow. Sometimes our days change, or sometimes someone is sick. Sometimes cereal is poured and we discover that I forgot to buy the milk. We change and postpone plans and they nearly never have a hissy-fit about a change. As adults, we struggle with change daily. We resist and go kicking and screaming into our next life phase while children just bounce, skip, and gallop ahead to what is next.

4) **Forgiveness**. They forgive so much better than adults do. Sometimes I am not patient. Sometimes I don't respond with love or generosity. Some days I am not a great mom. Sometimes I YELL! When I do, they forgive me quickly. If I notice I was short in my language and apologize, they instantly forgive me. And even if I don't

notice my error, they are not vindictive or mean. They do not hold grudges against me. They truly accept me as I am with all my many flaws and mistakes and continue to love me through it all. Forgiveness is one of my weakest areas, and I watch them with awe when they apply it so generously.

5) **Realness.** I have my own "special" bond with both of my kids separately. With Drew, it's humor. We have the same weird sense of humor. We look at each other after a six-hour marathon of Food Network and say, "How did this happen?" With a hand-formed "L" plastered on our foreheads, I respond "It's maybe because we just couldn't find the remote?" And then we belly laugh hysterically. With Ethan, it is our cuddle time. He values our couch cuddle time so much it has to be a part of his night to feel right. They each have a real and uniquely individualized bond with me. When they are real about who they are, it strengthens our connection. Why, then, as adults do we put on so many masks and waste our time morphing into untrue versions of ourselves?

6) **Humility.** When I first told Drew I had started a blog to practice my writing, I think he laughed for ten minutes straight. "What on earth will you write about, Mom? Are you going to tell everyone about your workout of the day?" Nothing like kids to remind you to not take yourself too seriously. As adults, we seem to lose sight that mistakes happen and, really, who cares? Take risks and learn from falling down. Many of the things we do as humans are

downright hilarious. Take the pressure off. Give yourself fully just as you are to this world knowing it's all going to be okay. The world will not fall if you don't get something right the first time or any time, but why not try something new to grow?

7) **Hope**. When they were younger, they were nearly one-hundred percent sure that we had the winning cereal box or waffle box that would give us a free family vacation. Now they still seem to have that hopeful dream that something great can come true at any moment. Any dream has the possibility to come true. Drew showed me an iFunny clip he had put together, and how it had made it to a certain level of "likes" online. If it continued to be liked even more, it would be one of the Top Ten Features of the week. I was so proud of him just for creating something that was of meaning to him and believing that he really could be the one that came out on top. Hope is everything. To me, hope means that little part of you that says, "Maybe today is the day. Maybe today will be the day my dreams and prayers are answered," and believing in that enough to move forward with an energy and lightness in your heart that accelerates yourself with love.

Being a mother is by far the greatest gift I have ever received. Each day I am with my boys, even the most frustrating, tiring, and weary of days still bring a soul-level joy to me. Some days I still can't believe I was chosen by God to be their mom. There is nothing perfect about my kids, me, or anyone. Yet, when I pay attention to how they do life differently than we do as adults, there is a lot we can learn just by watching them.

Spend a little time today tuning into the children that are a part of your life. Try to glean some new lessons from them as they live life as kids do. If we all slow down and pay a bit more attention to the children in our lives, we can certainly find a more beautiful peaceful way to live – the way we were destined to be when we came here before we learned how to be adults.

We not only need to have a deep respect for children; but also a deep respect for the child in everyone. — C. JoyBell C.

JOURNAL PROMPTS

How have you witnessed children teaching adults lessons instead of the other way around? What have you noticed that they do differently than adults?

Why do you think that adults find love more difficult to give and receive than children do? Where have you set limitations and rules around love that could be lifted to apply more acceptance and flow?

Select one of the seven ways to love that you particularly struggle with. What can you choose to do differently today to open up in a way that lets you love better?

DAY NINETEEN

WISH I KNEW THEN

I had a girl's night out this week to wish a great friend goodbye before she moves across the country. Four of us met for drinks, appetizers, and goodbyes. Our ages range from mid-thirties to mid-forties, and we have all been close friends for several years. We have all gone through our share of losses, changes, and broken dreams. At one point in the chattering and banter, someone said, "Boy I wish I knew in my twenties what I know now."

This is a common thought for people my age. Wouldn't that be nice? How great it would be to have avoided all the missteps, mistakes, and painful times? If you could just magically know as you were coming into being a woman in your twenties what we know now at this age....

Or would it be that great?

After I thought about it for a moment, I said, "No, I wouldn't want to know. If I had been mystically gifted with the knowledge of a forty-year-old woman, I wouldn't be the same woman sitting here right now. This journey made me."

Those mistakes, those struggles, and all the loss have formed who I am at my core. Those mistakes bore me the gifts of compassion and understanding. I could not be who I am today without the same journey.

As humans, we can't even hold certain spiritual truths in our hands until we are gentle enough to carry their weight. Age doesn't make you ready. Your life experiences make you ready. Those losses give you the ability to weigh for yourself what is important in this life. The lessons give you the ability to treat others with compassion and forgiveness. Our life lessons are not just learned, they are genetically and organically grown into our souls similar to the cellular changes taking place in your body.

So, while it might seem like a slick, easy thought to have been smarter when we were younger, there really is no shortcut to forming your soul into its destiny.

We should remember that when we are teaching our children. They have to go through their own pain and loss to form and shape their soul. They have to go through their own personal journey to become the form they were destined to be.

We can be there, be present, and give love without limits. But only they can shape their soul into their personal destiny through the road that they choose.

Retrospect: the sweetener of life.— *Kamand Kojouri*

JOURNAL PROMPTS

If you could go back and talk to your twenty-year-old self, what would you say?

What areas of your life did you have to learn the hard way? Do you think it was possible to learn those lessons any other way? In what ways do you interfere with others learning their lessons the hard way? Is that the best choice for them?

Who in your life deserves your gratitude for trying to steer you onto the right path in life? Write them an unexpected, sincere letter of thanks.

DAY TWENTY

DREAM HOUSE

It started as a clipping from a magazine – once our dream, now a reality now stood before me. We did this. Stick by stick. Step by painful step. Months and months of missing events to build the dream. Green roof, gray siding, topped with cedar shakes. Walls of glass facing the lake. Tress in all, eighteen had to be removed to nestle our dream in the woods by the lake. My boys grew up there. I rocked for hours upon hours in the nursery. Baths and suppers, swimming and praying, exploring in the woods. All was happy by daylight, but at night in the dark, the truth settled among the covers.

Not connected. Not one. A shell holding it all up until the weight of the truth was too much. Exposed. Broken. Unfixable and over. The beauty remains a dream nearly realized.

When you ask divorced people what happened, the answer is often the same: "We just grew apart." "It happened over several years." Not very settling, is it? Why? How does that happen, people want to know? It seems like a mystery to fall out of love as much of a mystery it is to fall in love. Unlike falling in love, which normally happens with a surprising suddenness, falling out is more gradual.

Little clues start seeping in the rafters. Feelings of no longer being understood or even known at all by the one you thought knew you the best. A feeling of not knowing the person who shares your home. You manage through it, mostly. Years and years go by. You do the best you can.

There are jobs to do, a mortgage to pay, and kids to raise. Perhaps you think it's a bit selfish to wish for more. You feel broken and useless. More years go by and the emptiness remains. How could we have attained so much together and then lost what brought us together? Like sand from the beach below our house slipped between our fingers – disconnected, dissatisfied, exhausted from trying. And then, the years go by. You start to hear the clock. Around age forty, something does happen to you.

This isn't a rehearsal. You have one shot at this life. What if we are hurting each other more than helping? What if the signs are telling us there's more? What if I am really incapable of making this other person happy? Ever, no matter what I do? Can I keep beating up against the same wall, having the same broken issues for yet another decade? Why does what I naturally am able to give create such a gap here? What if I'm really not enough here and never will be? It's killing my spirit to fail at such a crucial part of life.

I had resorted to living a fake shell of a life, going through the motions in a numb state of being, and eventually it broke me. I could no longer hold it up and hold it all together. I realized I was bitter and angry all the time and my boys didn't even know the real me. I wasn't by nature edgy and sharp, grumpy, and distant. I used to laugh and dance! Where had that girl gone to?

I will forever carry guilt for causing pain in the lives of loved ones, especially my boys. But I felt I had to give the old me a chance somehow to find her way back. I felt like I'd killed her myself. Divorce is cruel and awful and you can never anticipate how painful it is. While I wouldn't recommend or wish it to anyone, I am glad that on the other side of that painful divorce, I did experience growth beyond what I knew was possible.

I put on comedy shows in the kitchen, cooking dinner as if it were a HGTV cooking show or a Saturday Night Live skit, and I was the host with a British accent. Not even for just a few short snippets, but through serving the entire dinner – dancing and being crazy with my boys. My laughter returned. My joy surfaced again.

Drew often says, "Mom, you are the most different person I've ever met."

"What do you mean, different?" I ask.

"Just different. You are just sooooo unlike anyone else I've ever met. You are just very different than most people, Mom. Don't you see that, how different you are?"

My heart smiles. I know that he sees and knows the real me, the weird, unfiltered, qwerky, awkward, witty, jagged, and flawed. The real me. The me I was not able to find for several years.

Friends begin noticing that I actually do talk, and they mention that they feel more comfortable around me than ever before. When it all falls apart, there is nothing to force any longer. There aren't any balls to keep juggling. It has all fallen apart, all around you. You accept it all. All the dashed dreams and disappointment. All the pain and not fitting in to the group anymore. Failing the expectations of others. All of it. Embraced fully as, *yes, this is where my life is right now.*

Even my boys comment that they can't remember me really laughing or being so silly in the old house. I'm not saying there weren't happy times there; there certainly were. But something stifling and spirit-killing was happening to both my ex-husband and me.

I'd never call fifteen years and two beautiful boys a failure by any definition I consider that chapter of life a success in many ways, regardless of those that find it so easy to judge as a failure from the outside. I've found that those most likely to judge my path are the ones holding onto the most fear in their own lives.

It's easy to see things in black and white with sides to take. Judging is safe. It has a known outcome. There is someone to blame for the pain life holds. It's when you take down your guard and try to understand others who are different than you that's when it gets messy…and scary. And that's okay.

I would never blame anyone but myself for letting the essence of me die. I made the choice to disconnect and go through the motions instead of facing the pain. After it all, my advice to anyone wanting to avoid a divorce is the same thing they taught us in kindergarten. I apparently didn't learn it very well.

Just be yourself. Always be true to yourself.

Do not sacrifice any parts of who you are no matter how small for the sake of keeping peace. You were made who you are for a reason. If you are forfeiting pieces of you to make it work, it's either going to kill you or explode in your face under the pressure. Be true to you. If you need alone time, take it. If you need more time with friends, take it. If you need to explore a crazy dream you have, go after it. Own what is true for you.

These things I just listed are not *gifts* your partner allows you or permits you, or "lets" you do. These desires are who you are at your very core. There is no erasing who you are. Piece by little piece, erasing parts of you will eventually kill you. Nurture yourself first before trying to give to another.

There is a very fine line between compromising and completely giving up on yourself. You can't get water from a dry well. Get real with yourself and your partner now on an emotional, spiritual level. Glossing over the mess won't make it go away.

Now I feel more real than the Velveteen Rabbit himself. It feels rough and messy and out of my control at times. But I *feel*.

I had lived shoving away my feelings for so long that I simply longed to feel something again, to feel human and real, even if it meant that pain was the feeling. The point of being human isn't always pretty, and I love that part now with my whole soul.

You may not control all the events that happen to you, but you can decide not to be reduced by them. — Maya Angelou

JOURNAL PROMPTS

What beliefs do you hold about your role currently in your most intimate relationship that do not resonate with you? Do you believe you must hide or downplay any parts of who you are to make your partner happier?

How honest are you with your partner about your needs, whether they are needs you have from them or needs you have outside the relationship – to have friends, explore hobbies, have time alone, for example – without one ounce of grief or hesitation?

How do you support your partner in encouraging them to spend time on themselves and their interests, even when those don't involve you? Does jealously or envy show up, or are you able to encourage them to explore and express themselves without exhibiting an ownership mentality when apart?

What conversation would be most opening to your relationship? Below, journal some thoughts that you'd like to share with your partner to open that communication, and at the bottom, commit to a day and time you will have that conversation.

DAY TWENTY-ONE

WE ONLY EXPERIENCE LIFE THROUGH OUR THOUGHTS

Take a minute to think about that statement. Every single thing that happens to us is filtered into our brain through thought. Thoughts settle into our experiences. What shapes our history is based on what we think, and therefore what we feel about what we experience. This turns into what we feel about ourselves and what we feel about others.

When we encounter a rude, yelling person who cuts us in line at the shopping mall on Black Friday or at the grocery store on pre-turkey Wednesday, the thoughts we layer over the experience form and shape our outlook on the world.

We can either think, "Man, this world is filled with mean and nasty, horrible people that I need to protect myself from. I must learn to be more aggressive to protect my rights." Or, we can think, "Wow, there are just a lot of hurting people in this world carrying around a ton of pain that is hurting others. I wonder what I can do to help?"

What we think about our experience then determines the entire direction of our actions. Which direction do you want to go? Which direction helps make the world a more caring, loving place? The thoughts you allow directly cause your actions. You have to think about what you will do before you do it so that the thought naturally precedes the action.

If we want to be choosing different actions, kinder actions, more loving actions, we need to change our thoughts. Only loving thoughts can create loving actions. Ugly thoughts create ugly actions, and anything in between. Where do you want to live from?

And just think, we get hundreds of chances to choose the nurturing, peace-filled fork in the road every single day – with the thoughts you apply about your job, the unwashed dishes in the sink, the frowning store clerk, your silent sullied teenager, the car that took your parking space, the bills in the mailbox.

Everything that comes at you calls for a decision to be made. Positive or negative? Be thankful for all that is or carry a chip on your shoulder for all that is not? See the pain and offer tenderness or see only anger to be met with anger?

It is so powerful to think about all of us walking around with the world coming at us, and we get to choose what to do with it. Turn yourself into a stream of peace running through the chaos that shines a light for others to follow.

Did you know that you can talk back to that voice in your head? When the voice says, "That person sucks. They cut you off in traffic. Who do they think they are?" – you can answer inside as well. You can say, "Oh, there you go again. Thoughts floating around making up stories about people again. If you want to make up stories, how about this one? What if they just got news that their spouse has cancer? How's that for a story?" Think about it. Your brain is constantly throwing these stories together with no fact or basis in truth whatsoever. Why not just throw a different random story together with a more positive slant? It's likely to be about as accurate as your first story.

While constantly crafting a story about the information we take in around us, our brain wants to make the world make sense to us and make us feel as good as we can feel about ourselves. This often means we think the worst of others because playing victim is an easy role. We get to feel good about ourselves and aren't expected to really do much to change our situation. Didn't get the promotion you wanted? It must be due to that jerk boss of yours. That is a much easier story to live with than telling ourselves that we don't have the qualities they are looking for.

Think about what your brain does when you hear a bump in the middle of the night. Fear grabs a hold of you. Adrenaline rushes your body. You are suddenly consumed and zoned in on only, *what was that noise and where did it come from? Am I in danger?* Your flight or fight instincts that keep you alive are being activated. You may grab your phone or something for self-protection. You may even explore your house or flip on lights and peer outside. All of these actions were trigged by the fearful thoughts. You are on a mission to change your emotion of fear and seek out an explanation that your brain likes to help it feel better. You know what it's like to be in this moment. Your senses are heightened and you are on edge. That is the power of thought.

In this extreme example, it makes sense because we want to protect ourselves, but this same thing happens day after day all day long to a lesser degree each time you let a thought take you away. You let thoughts grab hold of your emotions and lead you down a path of actions that may not serve you. You sometimes don't even know this is happening if you aren't able to practice paying witness to your thoughts without attachment.

You may have a stressful, busy day and mindlessly eat two pieces of chocolate cake that you did not intend to consume. Your brain wants to feel better all the time. It is looking for ways to feel better and uses thoughts that aren't always accurate to guide your actions.

Becoming more aware of this process will help you be much less reactive in your life and more intentional in the actions you choose.

One of the most powerful revelations we can have as humans is the true understanding that we are not our thoughts. So many people think that if they were to define their "self," that it mostly includes the activity that goes on in our brain.

How do you know that you are separate from your dining room table? It's not a trick question. You (self) have the ability to notice it (table) is separate from you. Because you can notice it as something different than you, you know it is not you. Do you notice your thoughts? Yes, you notice them sometimes, and if you are being mindful, you may notice them all day long.

Here is the key, though – because you can witness yourself noticing them, then you know you are not your thoughts. If you are separate from your thoughts, then you must not *be* your thoughts. You must be the object noticing them. Some call this the *noticer* or the *watcher*. You are the noticer. You can witness your thoughts all day long, and you should. You'll notice they can be nearly full-out crazy!

Try writing down as many thoughts as you can for a day, then evaluate them at night. How truthful are your thoughts? How much sense do they make? Are they consistent at all? How helpful are they to serving you or those around you? Once you realize how unreliable, unhelpful, and downright hurtful your thoughts can be, the power no longer resides with them.

You can notice yourself having thoughts that don't serve you and choose to replace them with thoughts that do. This doesn't have to be elaborate. For example, you can replace damaging thoughts with a simple, "Today, I choose love," or, "Today, I see the light in others."

This action alone will shift your entire energy level and what is attracted to you in this world. Light attracts light. When you choose to be a light to the world, more goodness and light will find you.

The soul becomes dyed with the colour of its thoughts. — Marcus Aurelius

JOURNAL PROMPTS

Spend some time sitting quietly, meditating. Even if you've never meditated before, just sit quietly. As you have a thought, simply notice it. Don't think anything positive or negative about the thought, but simply notice it as, "Oh, there is a thought." Try it again with the next thought. This is a practice to do daily. As you repeat this you can notice more fully how separate you are from your thoughts. Try practicing for three to five minutes, and journal the thoughts you witnessed. How accurate were they? How helpful were they?

Now imagine that those thoughts you witnessed were words someone you love deeply came to you with about how they felt about themselves? How would that make you feel, and what would you say to them? Would it pain you to hear the thoughts you tell yourself were running through your loved one's head as thoughts they think about themselves?

Think of someone you know who appears to be genuinely more positive than most people. Ask them if their attitude is intentional. Ask them if they were always like that or if they had to practice. Ask them for their advice on how they maintain a positive outlook.

DAY TWENTY-TWO

FOR A DOG'S LOVE

I see the greatest site on my way to work that keeps me smiling all day long. I almost stop and take a picture, but the gentleman may think that would be a bit odd.

I am driving down the two-lane highway on my way into the city where I work. On each side of me, farms and empty fields pass by my window. I remember as a child watching the planted rows of corn passing by the car window. They always appeared to look like a broom end to me when you looked down the rows and they brushed across your car windowpane view, wider at the road's end and narrower as you looked farther off up the rows. It is winter now though, and the fields are empty and brown. There is no green to break up the brown ground this time of year.

I come up to a farm house and an elderly gentleman is mowing his yard – riding on a big, wide, dull green, John Deere tractor – only there is no grass yet to mow. The grass is all dead and brown. It's

March in Iowa. Why is he mowing his lawn so early in the morning when the grass is dead?

Apparently, because his very large, furry best friend *loves* running.

He has his golden retriever on a leash and they are both going back and forth across the yard. The old man, with a smile covering his entire face, drives the tractor, and watches his dog run alongside him.

As the scene reveals itself to me, I realize this may be the only way this elderly man can walk his dog. I can't imagine him managing to control the large-bodied animal and keep up with his furry partner well by walking.

What a wonderful site this is to see. Instead of these two best friends letting age and frailty be a hindrance, a joyful new solution is formed that bonds the two even closer. And, I will add, brings joy to strangers passing by as well.

Lovely things surround us every day, waiting to be picked up and noticed. Waiting to be turned in your hands, heart, and mind.

Notice them. Share them. Hold them in your heart and feed your soul with them.

As between those who notice such things and those who don't, I prefer those who do. — Wallace Stegner

JOURNAL PROMPTS

Do you think if you witnessed this same scene you would have viewed it the same way? Are you moving slow enough in life to know you would have noticed it? If you would have viewed it differently, how?

How observant do you consider yourself to be of the world around you?

Have you ever felt like God was talking directly to you through a seemingly unrelated event in your life? How in tune do you consider yourself to be to these lessons? How many lessons do you think you miss by being too busy to notice them?

What can you do differently today to remind yourself to observe life with curiosity and an openness to witness the lessons?

DAY TWENTY-THREE

FEELING TOO MUCH

I f I had a dollar for every time someone told me I thought too much or that I overthink things, I'd be writing this lounging on my own private island instead of at my kitchen counter mid-snowstorm. I've always been someone who examines the world and is often deep in thought. Those thoughts are often difficult to explain to others, because I've learned over time that not everyone views the world this way.

Lately though, I've been going through a phase in my life where everything related to that area of who I am seems especially magnified, like a burning leaf under the handheld magnifying glass in the sunbeam.

The word *melancholy* comes close to the feeling I have, but that word is too focused on sadness. It's not just sadness as much as a feeling that all I feel is now being magnified; it's also the joy I feel that is coming more into focus.

All my feelings, magnified times a thousand. Every moment, the happy and the sad, seem to be shouting to me lately, begging me to notice and pay witness. My heart is feeling more exposed and sensitive than normal, if that is possible.

As my boys start to look like men, I catch glimpses of their baby faces and it startles me with shock at how many years have passed.

When I witness strangers coming together to help support my brother, whose daughter is fighting cancer, I feel overwhelmed with so much gratitude for the kindness of strangers that I want to hug everyone I meet.

When I have a simple evening dinner with my family, I want to reach out to my mom and dad, hug them so tightly and let them know that I enjoyed our time together immensely.

My heart is big, heavy, and sensitive beyond comparison for every period of life that I've experienced. Maybe this is growing up, growing old, or just becoming "real," like the Velveteen rabbit. I'm glad to be feeling everything that surrounds me so fully.

These weighty moments are like post-it-notes stuck to my bathroom mirror that remind me, "We hope you enjoy the ride. Make sure you are buckled in safely, keep your hands inside the car at all times. And most of all....Enjoy!"

Except there are no safety belts in life to keep you in place, and no track laid out to follow exactly. And it feels like free-falling at times.

You can't predict when they come, but I call them "measurement moments." You don't feel time passing day to day, but every so often you get a glimpse, a snapshot laid before you to deliver the message.

Your friend's kids who were learning to walk are suddenly of drinking age at a wedding. Babies you knew are now six feet tall. Changes in people's relationships. People called before you in death missing from life's special occasions.

It all comes together and weighs on you at once, reminding you to enjoy these moments, witness the love, and let joy lift you up like the wind. It's so weighty of a feeling and realization, and yet so light to know you're just passing through this wondrous, beautiful, crazy place until you arrive home.

You have those moments where you realize there simply are no words strong enough to carry the weight of the feelings rolling around inside of you. As you grasp to put it into a form that your mind can understand, you feel yourself struggling. It's like your mind is trying to use its muscle to lift a five-hundred-pound weight with these thoughts. It doesn't take long for you to tire of exploring such existential thoughts, and then your mind simply must release them due to the sheer weight.

If you try to wrap your mind around this life and all its meaning for too long, you soon come to realize you can't comprehend it all. There is a wall there that your brain can't break through, the pieces aren't something you can put together and fully understand. That's when you give it up to faith.

I am happy to feel more than what most people are comfortable with and happy to have grown into this phase of life. At times though, it feels like a weight I'd like to shake off for a bit as it gets in my way unexpectedly day to day. It slows my steps and redirects my thoughts to unplanned, unscheduled time. Maybe that's the point, the reason for the pull.

I need to plan on possibly crying or hugging at the drop of a kind word and be okay with being that person on the verge of reaching out unexpectedly. I believe that if you are willing to experience any emotion possible, you can achieve the impossible.

You are only limited by your unwillingness to experience discomfort. Emotions are guideposts on our journey, pointing out the way we need to go next. When we suppress them, bury them, or numb them with food or alcohol, we lessen their effect on us. We alter our journey by ignoring the signs.

Maybe that is part of my role here – to help others recognize our innate connectedness as a constant undercurrent in all we do, and to bring that to the surface in my little corner of the world.

But feelings can't be ignored, no matter how unjust or ungrateful they seem.— Anne Frank

JOURNAL PROMPTS

Have you ever been accused of being too sensitive? How about not sensitive enough? How did that make you feel?

How do you feel that your sensitivity has expanded as you've aged? Can you recognize times in the past that you feel you may have been more insensitive compared to how you might react to the same situation today? How do you feel about the person you were versus who you are now?

How comfortable are you with other people who show their emotions?

Do you ever find yourself to be frustrated with people who seem to create drama or emotion where you feel it's unnecessary? Is your frustration related to a time or place, or do you find yourself resisting emotions even in a private setting?

What emotions are you most uncomfortable feeling, do you most resist, and why do you think that is?

DAY TWENTY-FOUR

ROSH BUSHES

She taught me how to play Skip Bo and beat me solidly every time except once. She was elegant, graceful, and proud. I will remember many moments with Lucille, like the winter day we made chicken pot pie from scratch with whole fryer chickens. By scratch I mean even taking the whole chicken off the bones. Determined to use what was left of her hand function, I held the glass pie dish half on the counter, half tipped over the edge for her. I held it firmly so she could still press the dough in the "right" way. My way apparently "needed some adjusting," she had said.

I had the privilege of getting to be Lucille's hospice volunteer for over a year. She was my dear friend. I kept her Tupperware she gave me chicken pot pie in purposely and never returned it. *You know you love someone when you're sentimental with their Tupperware.*

Another winter day in my memory was a long afternoon of her directing the setup of her elaborate Christmas village. It took over two hours. I covered every surface in the formal living room from the grand piano to all the table tops. She could still talk back then.

On this day it was about the rose bushes. I know nothing of flowers. When Lucille directed me around the garden, I seemed more like a bumbling toddler than a middle-aged woman. My mom and I talked often of hydrangeas and spiralis or something of the plant language, but it never filtered into my brain to stick anywhere. My upbringing was of no help to the current task.

She sat in the shade pointing to each bush. I ran over to where she pointed, dragging the awkward hose behind me and pointing the spray where she directed. The hose had a yellow plant food attachment. She had directed me how to attach it to the hose so that the water would come out intermixed with plant food.

Was this helping? Was I of help to her? How can anyone help someone like Lucille?

If I had met her ten, even five years ago, I would have felt outclassed, out cultured, outsmarted, and inadequate as hell. Well, I guess I still feel all those things around her, but if I'd met her professionally before all this, I'd never have such presumption to think I could ever help such a woman.

The first time I came to volunteer, I said, "I will be coming every so often for visits to cook, play cards, and just keep you company."

She replied with no curtness at all, simply stating the fact, "As long as this works for both of us," letting me know that I wouldn't be coming back if the experience didn't work for her. She'd no sooner have someone put upon her now in her condition than when she was writing medical textbooks or lecturing to medical students about genetic research.

Genetic research. There's a time bomb. A time bomb within each of us resides. Clicking and ticking off the time we have, the bomb hides as our feet patter on the dirt here. We never suspect our own expiration date that's already been stamped into our DNA. A code stamped within our tissues hours after our parents made magic. Irreversible. Unknowable.

Ironic and cruel it is that the field of study that she called her life's work is what betrayed her. I wonder if the cells knew, whispering to her soul, "Come, study our invisible date of expiration." It was betrayal in creation. Gosh, how she must have felt. "Yes. Thank you Lucille for your hours deciphering genetic code and saving the freshly minted babies from disaster, but we can't save you. Sorry. Better luck next time. Thanks for playing."

She was just a tad frustrated with my slowness, I could tell. She made a noise to get my attention. She pulled the laminated sheet out of the space between her left thigh and the side wall of her wheelchair. She started pointing at the letter boxes with her finger.

"W-A-T-W," I said the letters out loud. I looked at her confused and she shook her head.

She started again.

"W-A-T-E-R," I said the letters aloud again. She made a motion for drinking.

"Oh, gosh," I said. "Water, yes, I will go get you some water."

I put down the hose spray handle and laid it in the grass. I rushed off to the house to grab a bottle of water. Nervousness found me immediately as I imagined her somehow falling out of her chair in the thirty seconds I was gone. I scurried back quickly. I twisted off the cap for her and stuck the straw in. I held it up to her mouth so she could drink. It was a burner of a summer day. She motioned for more and I continued to hold the bottle for her until she was no longer thirsty.

I continued revisiting all her rose bushes at least twice with the hose until she was satisfied. After I put the hose back, I pushed her around to the front yard. She stopped me at these three-tall unusual looking potted plants. She took out her letter sheet and pointed out more letters tell me the name of the plants. It was all still filed away in her brilliant mind, locked away, forever unreachable to anyone else.

She seemed tired, so we went inside and the nurse took over to get her eased into her chair to rest.

It was the day of my last visit, the day of the rose bushes.

She passed away about one week later, having forfeited only one day in bed to her disease. A victor, she was. She had Multiple System Atrophy (MSA), and to only give away one day of her life to it in bed was a true testament to her spirit.

She was determined to suck every last ounce of joy out of this life every single day, and she succeeded. It was an honor to be blessed by her friendship.

I would have to learn to live in a different way, seeing death as an imposing itinerant visitor but knowing that even if I'm dying, until I actually die, I am still living. — Paul Kalanithi

JOURNAL PROMPTS

Who in your life have you witnessed fight a terminal illness? What can you recall observing about their spirit that was unique?

How did you feel being around that person during their illness? If you knew them before their battle, how did they change?

How did you change from knowing them and knowing the battles they were fighting? What would you like to tell this person about what they taught you?

DAY TWENTY-FIVE

OUTRUN FEAR

I had done my share of team-building work exercises, but this next one was a totally new experience for me. It was not just out-of-the-box, but more like *let's explode the whole entire box just to see what happens for fun.*

I was told we would have to climb a forty-foot telephone pole using the metal stakes that were sticking out of the pole's sides. When we got to the top, the goal was to hoist your body up on and stand straight up on top of the pole. Once we accomplished that, we were to turn one-hundred eighty degrees and face a trapeze bar hanging about eight feet in front of us. Finally, we were to jump and catch hold of the trapeze bar and drop to a safe landing in a large net below. The entire time, we would be attached to ropes for safety, held onto by two of our co-workers from another location we had just met two hours ago.

By the way, the two people in charge of the ropes only received ten minutes of training on how to properly do rope belaying. *Great.*

We each got to take our turn at this feat in front of fifty people, all of whom worked at our company. Very few of us actually knew each other because we were from all over the country.

We were all at a certain level in the firm. In this leadership training program, we would be competing against each other to be part of the next partner class in the firm. So, the entire group to me was full of strangers. These people were also suddenly my peers *and* my competition in the program. Team-building at its finest.

The first person started up the pole. At first he looked steady, but about halfway up he just stopped. It appeared that he was hugging the telephone pole with his legs and looking down. And so, he's done. Down he jumps, putting trust in belayers to be competent. *That part at least looks good so far,* I remember thinking to myself, trying to rack up the positives.

The next person was up.

Many more people came one by one to the pole to find their destiny and see if they could finish the feat or not. Finally, it was my turn. Oh, boy. I decided to try not to think, just focus on moving. And move I did. Later I was told that it looked like I was racing up the pole, trying to set a time record.

I knew that if I stopped, fear could find a place to wiggle in and talk to my brain. So, I simply moved one foot ahead of the other up the pole's metal spikes as fast as I possibly could. I knew the top would be a challenge. When I got to there, I was disappointed to find that the metal spikes didn't go up high enough to make getting on top of the thing any easier than climbing up it.

I had to hike one leg up to set the bottom of my foot on the pole, my other leg fully extended – at least for me, being that I'm just a few inches over five feet tall – because that foot was so far below it resting on the last spike. Up I hiked one leg, placing that foot on top. This is where I had to make the leap of faith. I had to yank that other leg up by pushing off the last spike, ready to put it next to the first foot.

This resulted in an awkward squatting position. With both feet planted on the top of the pole and my legs still bent, you can imagine where all the weight was positioned – yes, butt in the air. My feet and hands were still on the pole in a lovely squatting gorilla look, creating an undesirable, uneven weight distribution at the top of a forty-foot pole. My hands needed to come off from the top of the pole.

I needed to stand up straight. I made the move quickly, sticking with my "quick is good" theory. I swear the pole started swaying five feet in each direction from my sudden movement. My entire body was trembling with uncontrollable shaking. Oh, fear found my brain all right! It would not be outrun, and it was here with a voice shouting, "You're going to fall! You are going to fall. Just give up now, you are about to fall!"

I heard someone shout from below, "Breathe through your feet!" I had heard this on others' previous attempts. It sounded touchy-feeling, ridiculous to me...*breathe through your feet?*!

Yet, I had to steady my violently shaking body somehow. I took a deep breath, imagining it coming from as deep down as the soles of my feet, then up through my torso until that one deep breath filled my lungs with solid air, working its way out to my limbs in a steady force to stop the violent shaking. My body became stilled. It worked! I took another breath like that with the same imagery of it coming from my feet and grounding me. The pole stopped swaying and suddenly stood still beneath me.

I managed to take baby steps, turning around, and facing the trapeze before taking a flying jump for it. I finished the exercise successfully.

I went on to make many great friendships and gain many insights during this two-year-long leadership program. I will never forget that day as a stand-out experience.

Not because I succeeded, but because I learned.

I learned that at some moment in time, no matter what you do or how you plan, fear will catch up with you. Something will happen unexpected in your life that will strike fear deeply into your heart, take your breath away, and make you shake and question things as if the ground is moving right beneath your feet.

It could be anything – the loss of a loved one, divorce, loss of a job or a home. We cannot anticipate what lies ahead. But I learned that you can recover.

You can get your calm back. You can take action. Most importantly, I learned that to conquer fear you may have to be open to trying something you've never tried before. You may need to rely on a community outside of yourself. Going it alone is not always the best option. You will need to work through your emotions, be honest about how they show up for you, and maybe even try something that sounds ridiculous to you at first glance.

If we want different results we have to act differently, and sometimes that means listening to other ideas with an open mind. If we open our minds, we can give new ways a chance to work in our lives.

Expose yourself to your deepest fear; after that, fear has no power, and the fear of freedom shrinks and vanishes. You are free. — Jim Morrison

JOURNAL PROMPTS

When is the last time you really pushed yourself outside of your comfort zone? What was it? How did you feel in the moment? How do you feel about that event now with hindsight applied?

How did you respond to your discomfort – physically, emotionally? How did you work your way through it? What helped you?

What is something you've always wanted to try, but fear has held you back?

How can you apply what you learned about fear from past experiences to face fear in this new area you'd like to try?

DAY TWENTY-SIX

HOPE ON LAYAWAY

Whaven Sydney pulled the car into the dirt driveway, she stopped for a moment after turning the key off in the ignition. With both hands on the wheel, she looked out into the overgrown, dandelion-filled yard which was scattered with sandbox toys, a couple of balls, and a half rusty bike laying on its side.

How did I get here? she wondered. *Really, how? I am thirty-four years old and feel like I'm fifty-four. I have three kids that I am certain I am screwing up, a second marriage that seems to be disintegrating, and just thankful to be working two crappy jobs.*

I had dreams, just like everyone else. I dreamed of running away from home, moving to L.A., and being an actress at one time. In high school, when I found out I actually did have some talent for science, I dreamed of going to college for pharmacy. Who knows, maybe I had it in me to find the cure for something big.

When you are young, you think that old people are the only ones who gave up on their dreams. You see them all around you, trudging through life day after same kind of day, angry, irritable, and mad at the world for sucker punching them in the gut. Some of them carry such heavy scowl lines that you can see their white anti-tan lines on the rare occasion that their faces relax in a peaceful state. I suppose robbing innocent wide-eyed children of their dreams must be the job of some soul, like the grim reaper, but a slower, more painful drawn out way of dying.

Sydney lowered her head to her hands on the steering wheel and sobbed softly at first. The pain she was carrying had seemed so unbearable lately, like it had gotten even heavier in the last year or that she had become weaker against it. Though, nothing had really changed.

That was the problem – nothing had changed. By that time, she had thought she would have found a way back to school to make something more of herself. But that was not her life; that was someone else's life. Tears fell freely, her face wet and hands moist. God, she hated it. She hated facing her children and feeling like such a failure. *How am I supposed to show them the way when I don't even know it myself? I am halfway through my life and I'm no further along in achieving much of anything than I was when I was eighteen. At least at eighteen I still had hope to move me along.* Hope.

Paper towels

Toilet paper

Milk

Dog food

Frozen pizza

That's the grocery list that set off this spiral of despair. Silly, huh? How can a short little list like that make me feel so worthless as a person? How can a woman my age not have enough in her bank account to buy such inconsequential items?

Sydney had pulled into the Kmart parking lot earlier that day. She had watched people who looked just like her and her family go in and come back out carrying bags of the items they needed or wanted. Simple enough.

Two days before at the same Kmart, a different woman entered the parking lot taking in the surroundings and noticing the families going in and out. This was not her usual shopping spot. Out of the black four-by-four vehicle tumbled two boys with her. After entering the store, they made their way to the Christmas aisle and picked out wrapping paper since they had run out before wrapping their presents a few days earlier.

Then, they wound their way back to the layaway section.

"What's lay-away again, Mom," asked the ten-year-old? The mom replied, "It's when you have the store set something back that you want to have but can't afford, and you pay for it a little at a time."

They had to wait in line behind a couple other people making layaway payments. The guilt started creeping in slowly as the little voice in her head said, *You bought too many gifts for the boys, so many that you ran out of paper to wrap them.* The flushed feeling started at her neck and worked its way up to her jaw and then her cheeks. Shame. *We have too much.*

Well, that's why you are here, she told herself, *to share and help.* But she knew it would never be enough for her to feel right. She did many things to try to feel "right," and mostly, they didn't work.

Their turn came at the counter. She told the cashier they were there to do Secret Santa shopping and could they look up a family with some toys and children's items. They selected two families and paid off their balance in full. The cashier and the helper thanked her and told her what a great thing that was, but the mom's heart still did not feel healed. Better for a moment, maybe, but still shame for the wrapping paper roll tucked under her arm.

* * * *

Back at the car in the driveway, Sydney's self-pity was interrupted by a soft knock on the window. She wiped the tears from her eyes and looked out to see her beautiful nine-year-old daughter jumping up and down with a smile that overwhelmed her dainty child features with gigantic exaggeration. "Mommy! Mommy! Guess what?"

Sydney couldn't help but let her joy overcome her despair. She opened the door, pulled her daughter into her arms, and let the beautiful joy and innocence of her child heal her.

"Mommy, the man from the store called!" she shouted in her ear. "We won! We won! He said we got our stuff for free!"

"What store? What did we win?" Sydney thought for sure that it was one of those telemarketing gimmicks.

"Kmart, Mommy, where we have our Christmas at?" her daughter answered. "Someone bought our Christmas for us, Mommy. Isn't that so nice of them?"

The fullness started in her chest again, working up to her throat and face until her eyes filled again. She hugged her daughter even tighter, looked up and whispered "thank you" to the sky.

Later that night, Sydney kneeled by her bed to pray. She thanked God for giving her exactly what she needed – hope. She prayed for the family that she would never know that lifted her up, prayed that they had peace and love.

* * * *

That same night, another mom on the other side of town tucked her boys in and prayed over them. She prayed for the families she hoped they helped today. She prayed that it gave them a light in their Christmas season and gave them hope for good things to come.

And she prayed for herself, that she would feel peace within her heart and feel worthy, to be enough.

Do your little bit of good where you are; it's those little bits of good put together that overwhelm the world.— Desmond Tutu

JOURNAL PROMPTS

When was the last time you gave someone a random act of kindness? What was it? How did you feel afterwards? What came over you that caused you to do this?

Have you ever been on the receiving end of a random act of kindness? If so, how did you feel? What actions, if any, did you take afterwards?

Brainstorm below a list of random acts of kindness you could easily do and commit to doing at least one this week. Commit to doing one each week for the rest of the year if you feel up to that large of a challenge. Just imagine the joy you could cause!

DAY TWENTY-SEVEN

GOD IS LIKE A PIPEBOMB

When my mom calls to tell me, I am in the car with Drew on our way to his dentist appointment. She is crying. It is *that* phone call, the one we all dread because we know something devastating is coming our way.

"It's Eden; they think she has leukemia," she manages to get out.

My head starts reeling. *Leukemia. Cancer. Eden? Am I hearing the name wrong?* I can comprehend the cancer, that someone in our family has cancer. But I can't wrap my mind around the name my mom is saying. It's the name that really has me stuck.

"Who?" I ask, waiting to understand.

"Eden," Mom repeats. "Eden is sick."

"Eden?"

"Yes, honey. Eden."

Eden is five. She is my brother's daughter. Eden is the picture of an angel. She is mischievous and she laughs her twinkly laugh. She has fair skin and white blond hair that is thick with curls. She looks like a fairy. She demands that her honey topping be swirled in a perfect spiral on top of her breakfast oatmeal. She is innocence and wonder, light and love.

"She's been sick and not getting better, so they did some tests. They are trying to get a flight home now for her to come back to the States for treatment."

My brother and his wife have been teachers overseas for over a decade, living in several different countries. They come home each summer, and we pack full a year's worth of fun and connection in those three months before they venture off again. They have lived a life by their own design and have inspired me to live my own dreams without fear.

It is about one week before I get a chance to be alone with my brother after the news. He and his family had taken two different flights from Saudi Arabia – the first for Eden and her mom, Emily, the second a couple of days later for my brother Joe and their older daughter, Sophia. They started off in Chicago then transferred to near where I live in Iowa.

We are alone in the car, my brother and me. The closeness of our relationship demands that I say something, anything that is honest and real. But what do you say to someone you love when their world has just been ripped to shreds?

I say, "You know, if you want to go somewhere and just punch things, break things, burn things, I will take you there."

He looks at me. I feel a bit crazy for saying that, so I try to explain a bit more.

"I don't know how you feel, but if I try to imagine it, I would want to kill someone for what is happening to my daughter," I explained. "I would want to break glass and smash cars with a baseball bat and then pour gasoline over it all and watch it burn to the ground. I would want the anger to come out. I would want to break things the way I've been broken."

I continue, "I can do that for you, you know? If that's what you need, we can do that. I will do anything. I mean, anything you need. I don't care how messy it is. Anything."

Tears start rolling for both of us. I find it to be so odd that some of life's deepest conversations take place in a car where both parties are mostly looking forward instead of at each other. I think it isn't by chance that these conversations often happen like this.

He responds that is exactly how he feels. When he got the news he felt full of anger and destruction and yes, he doesn't know what to do with it.

Fast forward, and now Eden has been through one year of chemo and plenty of ups and downs. She has had an unfortunate rare side effect to one of the major chemo drugs that she needs, causing brain scarring each time she receives that drug. Despite her being halfway through her treatment and the outlook being optimistic, my anger at God has not changed.

I still have faith, though, because I don't know how to live without it.

But it is still an open wound in my relationship with God. I try telling myself I don't need to understand it, that someday the reason reveal itself. But what reason can there possibly be for childhood cancer?

I try telling myself that God doesn't control everything about our human experience and we have free will. But whose free will chooses this? No one's. I try to apply the logic of picking our path here, but somehow that just feels like a slap in the face to my brother and Emily.

There is no good reason, but I still have faith. I can't live a life without faith. I need to depend on Him even if I feel that He is letting me down big time right now.

This is not a life experience that I can wrap a tidy little lesson around, not yet anyway. It is still an open wound I am trying to heal. I am witnessing great love and generosity from complete strangers this year that is altering my world in a way nothing else can.

I am learning many lessons this year that I wish God would deliver in a less destructive package. I am not shutting Him out despite my disagreement with Him over this. Maybe we can only learn some things through extreme means?

There is a song that has been resonating with me lately. In the song, he talks about God acting like a pipe bomb, a cowardly surprise left in the most benign of places, ready to destroy.

I used to think that God moved in small, subtle hints, giving us gentle pushes in certain directions for the way we were supposed to go. I thought if you paid attention and lived a good life, you could follow the path as you were nudged along, arriving safely at your destination with His guidance.

But now I know the truth, that sometimes He is not the masterful, slow, methodical planner that an architect may be. Maybe He gets impatient with us. Maybe it's part of His plan to get our attention. Maybe He's mixing and mastering and just seeing what will happen with His experiment. He decides we need to not move slowly, but to run for our lives with fear as the earth shakes below us.

I get it, God. You have my full attention. I would like to hold on with a death grip to everything I hold dear in this life. I want to hold onto my kids, my family, my friends. I want to feel the joyful moments soaking into my cells, changing me into your vision for me. I want to laugh until my face hurts and taste life's joy. I want to have my breath taken away with the beauty that surrounds me. I want to hold it all so tightly and closely so that it doesn't escape me, elude me, or pass me by. I want it all to be mine and to never change. I don't want it to blow up in front of my eyes and be replaced by loss, sorrow, or despair.

But the tighter my grip, the more I sense You reaching for the next trigger to loosen my tight hold and remind me that this is not my plan, not my experiment, not my house to build, and not my flower to grip tightly in my clumsy hands.

Yes, I see now, and yet I know that as soon as I think I see, you will remind me again.

I know nothing of Your plans. I can only pick up the pieces that shatter while looking for the beauty in the mess. And still, I have faith.

I believe in Christianity as I believe that the sun has risen: not only because I see it, but because by it I see everything else. — C.S. Lewis

FIGHT

Run little girl.
Fight little girl.
Be sweet, smile, charm them all.

Break it, smash it, burn it.
Kill it.
Set it on fire angel.

Sweet soft smile of light.
The coward hides inside you.
Ashamed.
Feeding off your innocence.
Covered with a sweetness to protect it.
Come out and fight.

We spin around, still moving.
Walking. Driving. Talking.
Shopping and weather and complaining.
People eating. People living.
The coward hides.

Words I never knew I never knew.
Hate. Anger. Destruction.

Run little girl.

Fight little girl.

Set it on fire sweet angel.

JOURNAL PROMPTS

Everyone faces loss and difficulties in life. You can't escape the journey without experiencing significant loss. What have been the greatest losses you've suffered so far in your life?

Have you ever felt let down by God in these times? How has that changed your relationship with Him?

How has your perspective over these losses changed over the years? How have those losses shaped you as a person? How have they affected your own faith?

How do you reconcile life's extreme losses with its great blessings? Do you think a person can experience the full blessings of life without the losses? Why do you think life is designed to come with so much pain?

DAY TWENTY-EIGHT

GRAB YOUR LIFE PRESERVER

I t was day three of our cruise. I had saved for over a year for this extra-special vacation with my boys – a seven-day cruise. Heaven. We had been waiting in anticipation for months.

There is yelling first, people yelling. I am standing on the beach, talking to the boys. When I break out in a full-on sprint, my plastic cup, filled with rum punch, falls to the sand. A splattering of red drink soaks in quickly.

"Help! Help! Help!!!!"

Click. React.

The big guy near me jumps up from the beach to help.

Click. React. Run.

"Help!" *Run.*

The big guy is in the water before me. I thank God he's as big as he is. He was a stranger only seconds before, but we're suddenly brought together in the same moment.

Click. React.

The old man's body is gray, white with a bluish purple tint. He looks dead already.

Click. React. I fall to my knees over him.

I look at the big guy. My eyes say I am ready, but my voice has left me.

Click. React. I'm ready to do the breaths. *Yes, I'm ready.* I'm at his head and he's laid out. *I'll do the breaths*, I say with my eyes.

Merciless tide washes over his face with more death.

Click. React.

I pull him higher, onto his side. Water escapes his blue lips.

Click. Ready. Let's go. I'm about to lean in. More death washes over him.

I jolt him up to higher sand. "Wait…" someone says.

"He's breathing."

Watch. Wait. Yes, it's the slightest lift ever, so tiny, so shallow.

His eyes flutter. *Watch. Wait.*

I roll him on his side. More water escapes.

There is more of a lift in his breath. More life shows up.

Watch. Wait. Faint color returns.

I breathe. I stand. He's breathing. Yes, he's breathing. Nine-one-one has been called to the island beach.

Later on, I ask my boys what all happened, unable to remember it all. They say that I was kneeling over him, rubbing his face, and talking to him. I don't recall all of it. *Click. React.*

Then later, the questions…the examinations.

What if…?

What if he hadn't started breathing?

What if I had done CPR?

Would it have worked?

Would he have died?

Did I do enough?

What if my training was more up to date?

I should take an updated class. How many breaths to compressions is it now? They have changed it, I know.

The old man, Bob – we learned his name during the event – had jumped into the ocean off the catamaran sailing boat. I remembered him. He and his wife had jumped in just a few seconds before I had. She had a noodle floaty. He had nothing.

I jumped in right after them, and felt that magic ocean rise as it pushed me to the surface – it always seems to take longer to surface than I ever expect. I swam straight in a line to my boys on the beach. Based on where Bob came out of the water, he must have swum left at a slightly different angle. If my boys had been standing more to the left, I would have been swimming closer to him. I shudder now to imagine what would have happened then – Bob and I both without life vests, he much larger than me. I could have been a gray one drug up on the beach, too.

I vow to take a CPR class again. I vow to grab a life vest, even if I alone can swim without one. How can I help another if I am not equipped for the "What if?"

I am reminded that my job here on earth isn't just to take care of myself, but to prepare myself to care for my brother. I need the life vest not only for me, but to enable myself to help more others as well. We can't stop the accidents that are surely part of the journey, but with preparation and humble admonition of our limits, we can surround ourselves with a life preserver to be used by us or by our brothers. It's of no matter since we are all one, all connected – one responsibility to all.

Chance favours the prepared mind. — Louis Pasteur

JOURNAL PROMPTS

What aspects of your life are you not paying attention to? Self-care? Your spiritual life? Health?

Things may be working just fine the way they are in your life, but what if something devastating and unexpected were to occur? Are you putting yourself in the best position to take on whatever comes your way?

Or, try looking at this issue in another way – do you keep your tank full? When your job, family responsibilities, and stress take their toll on you, do you take the time out to fill yourself back up? Or are you running on empty, hoping you have enough gas to make it? Do you hold the belief, whether they're false or not, that taking time for you is somehow selfish? Why?

What changes do you need to implement to achieve certain levels of stability and strength that not only allow you to save yourself, but others in your life?

DAY TWENTY-NINE

DO YOU HAVE A SOUL TRIBE?

When we are young adults and teens we tend to envy those who have seem to have so many friends. The high school experience alone can be viewed as a four-year-long popularity contest, culminating in who is named to the homecoming court. *Blech.*

As we grow into our lives, we come to realize that we only need a few close friends who hold special spots in our hearts. As life fills in with adult and family responsibilities, we also come to realize that we can only devote enough energy and time to support just that handful of special friendships.

The rest of the more surface-level interactions seem to gradually fall out of our lives. It's not that we don't still enjoy those acquaintances, but we don't devote our time to growing more of those relationships. Only a few special people hold spots in our soul tribes. They nurture our journeys, providing guidance and inspiration to us. They help us become the best version of ourselves. There is only so much time, and we need to focus on the friends who support us, know us well, and help us grow in your journey.

This gets me thinking about the kinds of friends we really need and who they are:

LIFELONG FRIENDS

We have known this type of friend for nearly our entire lives. Lifelong friends know us inside and out. The greatest part about these friends is that they understand us so fully. They saw us struggle with growing up. They know the families we grew up in. No explanation is needed for why we are how we are with these friends. They know this because they have witnessed so much of the creation and growth of who we are today. They "get it" without us having to explain a thing. Years can go by without significant time together, and it still feels like just yesterday when we are finally together.

WILD FRIENDS

These are the friends we call when you know you need a pick-me-up. Something blows up in our lives, and they are the ones we can count on to bring on the sparkle, laughter, and joy for at least one evening. They are the ones whom we often have to talk out of their crazy ideas. Wild friends make us laugh until our faces feel paralyzed from smiling so much.

PATIENT FRIENDS

These friends are our loyal confidants. They basically serve as our free therapists. These friends have listened to us percolate and contemplate our relationships, health struggles, career struggles, all of it. All of it over and over and over again. These friends show patience and love like no other. They are there for us no matter how many times we go back and forth on the same issue. These are our rock-solid friends.

BRUTAL FRIENDS

These friends will stop us in our tracks to keep us from lying to ourselves. Even if it hurts, they will speak the truth. Unlike the "Patient Friends," the brutal friends bring us to the solution quickly and without hesitation. The thing they realize, (and we do, too) is that we already know the right answers for our dilemmas. We just like to waste time avoiding the truth and postponing it because we know what it is, and we don't like the answer very much. We've given fear the steering wheel and we are just riding along. Instead of going bravely towards the path we need, we stammer and putter around until our pain becomes greater than our fear. "Patient Friends" can turn into "Brutal Friend" when they're frustrated watching us hurt ourselves.

PASSION-ALIGNED FRIENDS

These friends share our passions and love to talk about them with us for hours. They connect with us in our life's passions – spiritual growth, yoga, cooking, books, whatever our passions may be. When we get together with them, we share ideas and help each other grow in love for our shared passions. Not everyone understands our passions, but these friends do.

The best part is that all of these types of friend needs we have can be filled by just a very few friends. Even one person can fill all of these different friend needs for us depending on the relationship.

One of the greatest things about getting older is that we come to know who our true friends are. Maintaining and growing those relationships is not an effort, but pure joy. With age and maturity, we release the need to be at all the social events and to be friends with tons of people. It is much more satisfying for us to explore the depths of our friendships instead of the breadth of many friends.

She was a collector of reflections looking for souls that could see deeply inside her soul. — Shannon L. Alder

JOURNAL PROMPTS

If I asked you to name your soul tribe, who would be in that group?

Think back over the last month. How much time did you spend with people who truly enrich your spirit and life?

In the same period, how much time did you spend with people who drain your soul of energy or who feel like more of an obligation to keep up with than a joy?

What reasons do you have for investing time with people who drain you or don't lift you up? How can you make more time for those rich relationships that match with your vision for your life?

Role play in your head – how will you say no to the next invitation that comes your way that doesn't feel enriching to you? How will you gracefully say no? What consequences do you need to prepare for to make that transition to making more time for your soul tribe?

DAY THIRTY

KNOCK DOWN

I t comes from nowhere in a way we can never possibly predict. Boom. Our lives change just like that and our views are suddenly from the floor. We're knocked down, right off our feet in an instant.

Even though we've been knocked down and our heads are reeling, we still try to make sense of what hit us. *Where the hell did that come from? How did I not see this coming? Was my back turned? Why me?*

After all of the questions, only one answer matters. Our only option, our only answer, our only choice, is to get up off the floor. We dust yourselves off, hold our heads up, and keep going.

We just keep going.

One of my life truths is that if you are still here and still breathing, there's a reason for your presence. There's a purpose you need to fulfill yet. No one else but you can fill that purpose.

We're not done yet, no matter how tired we feel, no matter how heavy our hearts. We have important work left to do here.

I believe that on good days.

But do I believe it from the view of the floor?

We get up off the floor, dig our feet in, stand tall, and give it yet another go. There is no such thing as failure unless we give up our hope.

It's not always pretty, and sometimes our efforts seem to yield disaster. We wonder if what we are doing really matters. We know that life is full of knock-down hits. We know the hits are coming and we realize we're not immune. They still knock us over solidly and swiftly when they come, no matter how aware we are that this will happen.

Sometimes life requires more of us than we feel we have within. That's when God picks us up and shows us how big we really are with Him. We grow to realize that we do have all we need to not just endure our trials, but to use them to make ourselves and the world even more beautiful, more full of light.

The view from the floor after a knock down isn't permanent. There is no other way, no other option than to stand up strong, find your fragments of hope remaining, relocate your faith, and get ready to grow big.

There should be a word for how pain can also be beautiful. I guess there is – life.

Tonight, I am attending a fundraiser dinner with some fabulous ladies to raise funds for helping victims of domestic violence. We all chipped in and bought out a table. Our money going towards a good cause, we are so happy to give. But as I was journaling this morning, I noticed that instead of feeling like I am giving I feel like I am receiving.

I am overwhelmed with gratitude to be in the place that I am now. I still remember nights on the bathroom floor in agony, praying for the pain to somehow, in any way possible, end. I remember feeling that there was no way out of my experience with domestic violence. And here I am twenty-five years later the other side. I thank God for taking a broken vessel like me and showing me the way out. I thank Him for the experience that allows me to feel compassion without judgement for other women facing the same thing. Here I am in a place where I can help, all because He picked me up off the floor, dusted me off, healed my wounds, and showed me how to grow bigger.

When people learn about that early chapter of my past, they often comment about disgust towards the abuser. I am thankful that I have found forgiveness – forgiveness for myself, forgiveness for him. It was only a couple of years ago that a friend of mine saw him somewhere and he asked her to give me a message. His message contained a few things; one, he wanted to say how sorry he was; two he wanted me to know that I saved him; and three, he wanted me to know he thinks of me often and wishes me nothing but the absolute best that life has to offer.

I don't know why that was part of my life path, but I accept it fully. I can honestly say I wish him nothing but the best, also. I will leave you with one more life thought that I believe with all my heart: People are truly doing the best they can. Even with all the ugliness around us, I truly believe that everyone is doing the best with the tools they currently possess. I was doing my best back then in that abusive situation. I was doing my best in my fifteen-year marriage. I am doing my best now. My best just gets better as I learn from my journey, and I remain open to growing into a new best.

I hope you can see that too in this world. See the best in everyone, even if it doesn't look all that pretty on the surface. The world is a kinder place to be in when you believe this.

If your heart is broken, make art with the pieces. — Shane L. Koyczan

JOURNAL PROMPTS

When has life felt like a sucker punch to you? What happened that knocked you down?

How did that event change you as a person? How did it change your trust and your connections to others?

How have setbacks in life made you a more compassionate person?

When you've been knocked down hard, who can you identify in your life that you can call for help and hope from the floor?

Who can call on you for the same type of support? Have you told them they can call on you for this?

DAY THIRTY-ONE

JUDGEMENT KILLS COMPASSION

I still think about it at least once a week. It didn't even happen to me. It happened to strangers on my street. The most awful thing. A toddler died.

How it happened, even more awful. The condos are interconnected. An extended family had gathered together for a weekend of early Christmas celebrations. Somehow an eighteen-month-old girl and older sister around age three or four were left alone in the tub. Somehow the water that was off got turned back on. Somehow the toddler fell and was under the water. Somehow the screams of the older girl weren't heard. Somehow the people responsible forgot. Somehow no one else asked. Somehow the minutes missed were the wrong ones.

When you first hear of a story like this your heart rips in two. How could this happen? What could have taken the attention of the parent in charge? Why couldn't they hear the older girl? Why didn't anyone notice? Why didn't the older girl run for help? Why? How?

Then it all turns to anger. There should be answers. A little girl is dead. An entire beautiful life lost to what, for what? Someone was in charge. Someone had a job to do. They failed at a simple job of don't leave a toddler alone in a tub. Even my teenage boys know this simple rule. I told my kids about what happened as I didn't want them to hear about it from someone else. Their reaction was also sickness, sadness and mostly anger.

I spent maybe a day and a half in that state. Looking for answers and someone to blame for life's cruelty. It wasn't until that Sunday night that my judgement finally made room for something else.

Compassion. Where was my compassion?

There was a family just houses down from me in the deepest pain and despair that anyone could ever experience. Instead of reaching out to show compassion I sat alone in judgement. Is that what God called me to do? I don't think so. I believe anytime we judge another it comes from fear.

We know we ourselves are just as human and mistake-prone as the person we are judging. Judging is our attempt to separate ourselves from them so we can protect our own ego. That would never happen on my watch. I would never have done such a thing. Judgement makes us feel safe in a dangerous world. It's a cop out.

I did not reach out to them that day. I felt it was too late, too private. Truth be told it was probably too scary for me and I let fear decide. I will always view my reaction to this situation a lesson for me, and a failure for me personally. I don't know what I expected out of myself, or what I thought it would do in terms of helping. But I do know that more is expected of me than what I did do. I could have shown the stranger down the road cared about their pain. I did not.

So, now whenever I hear that voice of judgement I let compassion tap it on the shoulder and tell it to step aside. You are not welcome here. That is not what this is about. I try to let compassion take the lead and notice when judgement seeps in.

The main message of Jesus, I believed, is that mercy trumps justice every time. — Paul Kalanithi

JOURNAL PROMPTS

Identify a time you have judged or listened to another being judged. Examine what was being judged? What fear did it touch in you that you can relate to the reaction to judge?

Think of a time when you showed more judgement than compassion or empathy. What good came from the judgement if any? What would you say to that person today if you had a chance for a do-over?

Today notice your own judgement and the judgement of others. In conversation there are plenty of judgements passed around. Practice identifying why the judgement arises in the situation.

What fear is at the core of the need to judge? How can you approach these situations in conversation by bringing more compassion to redirect the thoughts and conversation?

DAY THIRTY-TWO

A DAY INTERRUPTED

I was on my way to a meeting, and despite running an errand first, I still looked to be on time. I was coming from a direction of town I normally didn't drive from, so was kind of winding my way the direction I wanted to go.

I came upon a funeral procession coming my way, so I pulled over. I am unsure when people stopped pulling over for funeral processions, but I still do. I would feel extremely disrespectful not to.

I really didn't think anything of it at first. I checked my phone, looked at the time, changed the station on the radio. Then I started noticing truck after truck with the same business logo on it. Red ones, white ones, all from the same business. Then a related business name on more trucks. A related company in a similar field maybe.

I started noticing how long this procession was going to be. There had to be hundreds of cars and so many trucks. I saw four different police cars just in my area playing tag team and running up the line. They were trying to keep the line together and not let other drivers interrupt their unity. I even saw one police officer scold some driver trying to interrupt the flow to make his turn.

I was still on time and not concerned. I don't tend to get worked up about things like this, so it's always interesting to me to watch people just unravel when these things pop up in life.

I thought to myself *Who is this person who has touched so many lives?*

So being in a smaller town, I searched online obituaries with the company name I'd been seeing in the search. I don't know this individual, so I won't share the name, but I was suddenly transported to a feeling of deep respect and love, awe even. The man these thousands of people had gathered to say goodbye to was a father, a coach, a business owner, a man who believed in God and showed that faith it was said in multiple ways to many people.

He was said to be extraordinarily generous. He died pursing a hobby he had a passion for. He was five years younger than me. I just kept looking at all the cars and trucks passing me by filled with people that loved him. A life lived well. Love spread abundantly. Light that touched others. Passions pursued fearlessly.

I felt blessed to have that moment to witness such love and be forced to sit with it for as long as it took the cars to go by. Forced to feel the emotion of it, the realness of it.

I was thankful I took that winding, unintended route through town that day. Grateful for the message delivered to me, and happy to be late for my meeting.

I had somewhere more important to be. Sitting in my car, witnessing love go by one by one, with their headlights on.

Tell me, what is it you plan to do with your one wild and precious life?
— *Mary Oliver*

JOURNAL PROMPTS

Think back to the last time your day got completely off track. Did you face it with resistance or acceptance? Were you one of the stressed-out car drivers in the story trying frantically to get around this mess and get on with your day? Or were you more like the writer, letting the new plan take hold of your day?

Identify a time you did resist a change in your plans. What do you think you may have missed by resisting instead of embracing presence?

What mantra or self-talk can you put down on paper to fall back on to remind yourself next time to embrace the mess and look for the messages trying to reach you?

DAY THIRTY-THREE

PSST...YOU ARE THE HERO OF THIS STORY

B eing human means facing some pain and suffering in your life. If you have no suffering, just wait. You will.

You could have a parent slipping away before your very eyes from Alzheimer's Disease. You could have experienced sexual abuse. You could have a child facing cancer. Grown up in an alcoholic home. Grew up poor. Lost one of your parents at a young age. Felt geeky and out of place your entire life. Lost all your retirement. Never had a chance to go to college. Been in a horrible car accident that left you disabled. Facing a chronic disease that will be part of your entire life.

The list is endless. Every single one of us will have some pain that holds the power to define us. To nearly overcome us. To shift the very earth we stand on. Those events could be behind you, and we all know there may be some in front of us still.

The question I have for you is...

Do these events define you?

Have you let this truth somehow seep deep into becoming an identifier of who you ARE? Do you make this part of the explanation you give yourself or others for why life hasn't turned out as good as planned?

Does it limit your potential? Do you define yourself as a victim of abuse or alcoholism? Do you make it part of who you are today, holding onto it like a constant companion, ingraining it into your very being? Wear it like a label stuck on your shirt?

But, that IS who I am you may say.

Is it? Is that what you are at your deepest core? You are this pain and suffering? Is that what God sees in you? Is that what you want to be?

How much more power do you want to give this event?

The pain from a trauma has to be faced and worked through. The emotional work of these painful events is real and there are no short cuts.

Needing help to get through the pain is also part of being human. Trauma changes us. We are a different person than who we were before trauma.

But eventually don't you want to do more than just barely survive that which tried to take you down?

Whenever you decide you are ready, another character in the story besides victim is available for you to own. Spoiler alert for those that haven't reached the end of the book yet, but YOU are the hero of this story. YOU are the hero of YOUR story. You weren't born to be cast as the victim. YOU my dear are the freaking hero of this story! Didn't you know?

You can never be the same as you were before the trauma, but you most certainly can be something even stronger, more beautiful, and compassionate than you ever imagined. You can do more than just endure and define yourself by the trauma. You have the power to transcend and transform your life after the trauma into whatever you want it to look like.

Dream big. Make it so beautiful it takes your breath away, and maybe even scares you a little bit. Maybe with what you learned you want to help thousands of people facing the same pain.

Go do it. Get to it. What would the hero of this story do next? How would they surprise everyone at the end of the story? Grab onto that. Be that story. Live that story. You have the power to recast your role in the story and change the ending. This is your story. Are you writing it?

Heroes aren't heroes because they worship the light, but because they know the darkness all to well to stand down and live with it. — Ninya Tippett

JOURNAL PROMPTS

What in your life history have you let attach itself to you, becoming part of your identity, part of your explanation for why you are the way you are?

Is that experience something you want to define yourself by? How is using that to define yourself helping you? How could it be limiting you?

Is there another version of the story about what happened to you that could prove more empowering in your life? Take a few moments and explore another angle to frame your history into that is more empowering than you thought possible.

Reread what you wrote. Does it stir something inside of you that you can identify with?

MY WISH FOR YOU

If I have but one hope for you it is this: I hope you slow down enough to notice and savor the moments. I hope you hear God's message He has designed for you. His message is all around you, every single day you are here. He is trying to teach you, to lead you in these everyday lessons.

That alone is all you need to do to set your own personal journey here on earth in motion. If you slow down enough to notice and get quiet enough to hear, you will hear your soul speaking to you.

Your soul already knows the message you seek. It was imprinted with the message before you were born, and it wants to let you in on the secret. Quiet yourself to hear it. Listen to what your soul tells you in those quiet moments of connection and truth, and follow that one step at a time. Trust the mapmaker's map for you. Embrace each lesson as one designed for you to guide and direct your journey.

You will find yourself exactly where you were destined to be.
You will find yourself by just BEing fully present right where you are.

In Love, Light and Faith,

Dawn

ACKNOWLEDGEMENTS

Thank you to anyone who has ever reached out to encourage me, and let me know that I have touched you. That is really the only reason to write for me. To share a connection, create a dialogue between the writer and the reader at a time, place, and emotional space neither one of us could predict.

I also had two wonderful editors help me with this book. Debra Engle and Michelle Barichello both contributed wonderful advice and insight. I would highly recommend working with either of these class act, amazing ladies.

And I thank God for blessing me with the ability and determination to work on writing as a craft. Much of what I write doesn't come from me as much as *through* me. Many times I will look back over my writing, not even sure where exactly it came from. I thank Him for allowing me the privilege to use my voice for good.

LET'S CONNECT

Join me on the journey of my next book. Find out when it will be available for beta readers and launch. The next book is a fiction novel inspired by a true story of a boy growing up without parents. Despite multiple arrests and incarceration, he finds something bigger reaching for him, and finds the strength to transcend his circumstances. This book will show you the power of the human spirit to overcome adversity, and how even those most different from you, are fighting the same exact battles you are here. The first draft is about half done and I am hoping for a 2018 release.

www.dawnmhafner.com

ABOUT THE AUTHOR

Dawn has worked over the past twenty years in the financial industry, leading teams, coaching employees, and providing client service. She started writing as a way of achieving balance.

Over her career, she had one theme that helped her find success and balance.

BE Where You Are.

She latched onto this phrase to guide her choices when she became a mom and struggled to balance work, parenting, and time for self. BE Where You Are means to truly embrace where you are in this current moment. We can only focus on what we are doing in the moment. Once we learn how to fully submit to the present, we can evaluate, and guide our compass towards where we want to arrive in the future.

Dawn lives in Iowa with her two teen-age boys. She reads everything she can get her hands on. She enjoys walks with her dog Grace, boating, fitness activities, and a little golf. She enjoys volunteering for Dress For Success, and 50% of the profits from this book will be donated there.

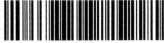
62657099R00125

Made in the USA
Lexington, KY
14 April 2017